A 1,000-Mile Walk on the Beach

A 1,000-Mile Walk on the Beach

One Woman's Trek
of the Perimeter
of Lake Michigan

by

Loreen Niewenhuis

"Life should be an adventure!"

CRICKHOLLOW BOOKS

Crickhollow Books is an imprint of Great Lakes Literary, LLC, of Milwaukee, Wisconsin, an independent press working to create books of lasting quality.

Our titles are available from your favorite bookstore.
For a complete catalog of all our titles or to place special orders:

www.CrickhollowBooks.com

A 1,000-Mile Walk on the Beach
© 2011, Loreen Niewenhuis

Cover photograph and design is by Philip Rugel.

Original Trade Softcover

To my sons, Ben and Lucas

May your lives
be filled with adventure.

Contents

Introduction

My earliest memory of Lake Michigan is of a six-year-old me running full speed down the mammoth sand dunes at Warren Dunes State Park, on the eastern shores of the great inland body of water. I'd race my siblings up the shifting hill, one step slipping back for every two taken. At the top, we'd turn and look down on the lake.

The Lake.

Blue water, on and on and on. There was no way to see the other side. It stretched left and right and forward till it met the sky. The breeze off the lake blew up the dune, warming and lifting from the hot sand.

Lifting.

There was so much rising air that hang gliders would launch off the top and glide high over the foot of the dune all the way to the water's edge, banking and stalling and turning. You could fly off that dune if you had the right wing.

We did the next best thing: we ran.

We ran so fast that our legs could not keep up with our bodies; we'd pitch forward, heels-over-head, and end sprawled on the warm slope. Once we caught our breath we'd continue the downhill race.

That exhilaration, that rush – followed by a plunge in the always cool lake – marked me, and I have been constantly drawn back to the shores of Lake Michigan.

When I turned 45, I felt something pull at me, goading me to take on something bigger than myself, to challenge myself in a big way. I considered long hikes on some mountain trail, but every time I contemplated weeks in the woods, I thought, *I will miss the lake.* Then it occurred to me: why not take on the lake? Why not walk its shoreline day after day until I had walked all of it, captured it in my muscles, recorded it in my body? Begin the adventure in Chicago and walk until the Windy City skyline disappeared behind me, then – months later – see the same skyline appear as I approached it from the opposite direction having fully encircled this Great Lake.

So, it was decided. In the fall of 2008, I told my husband, Jim, "Next year, I'm going to walk all the way around Lake Michigan."

He paused for a moment, then asked, "Well, shouldn't we discuss this?"

I simply said, "No."

It had been decided. It was the adventure that I must have.

I am a wife and the mom of two boys, Ben and Lucas. They were both teenagers when I decided to undertake the Lake Trek. I had worked in medical research when they were little, but was able to stay at home with them when my husband got his first job after residency. I enjoyed the privilege of being there for my boys, to pack their lunches, drive them around, be the mom who volunteered for things at their school. Now Ben had just gone off for his first year of college, and Lucas was driving himself to school. The nest was emptying.

It was time to take on something that would challenge me physically, emotionally, mentally. To take on something that could be completed instead of the household chores that never ended. I didn't think my husband would understand the need to do this. He's a steady guy. He has cold cereal every morning, and stirs it the same way. The sound of the spoon scraping the side of the bowl, lifting the cereal, then the bowl turning an exact partial turn on the countertop until it has made a complete revolution greets me every morning as I wait for the coffee to brew.

No, I didn't want to discuss it to death. He'd want me to justify it, to have it pass his test of being "necessary."

I thought about the piles of dishes and laundry, the meals I cooked almost every night, the taxiing of kids that I had done for years. I did not regret doing these things. But years of constantly giving can chip away at who you are, and it seemed like a good time in our family life for me to launch out on my own. I wanted to test and push myself, and to make sure I still knew who I was apart from my identity within my wonderful family.

The Lake Trek called to me.

That fall, I began jogging several times a week until the snow started falling. Through the winter, I trained at the gym. I built up muscle mass and dropped a few pounds. My stamina increased, and I began to feel stronger in my body.

Through the winter, I studied maps and satellite images of the lakeshore, the beaches, steel mills, oil refineries, major and minor cities, stretches of parks, the wild expanse of the southern edge of Michigan's Upper Peninsula. I decided to map out the coming journey in segments, sections to walk over four seasons.

And I decided to always keep as close to the water as possible.

I would begin and end in Chicago on the tip of Navy Pier, an urban peninsula that reaches over a half mile out on the lake. I would trek around the lake counter-clockwise, the lake always holding my left hand.

This is my journey that became *A 1,000-Mile Walk on the Beach*.

Walk with me.

Segment 1

March 16–20
Chicago, IL to Union Pier, MI
72 miles in 5 days

Total Trek Mileage: 72 miles

Heading to Chicago

To begin my hike around Lake Michigan, I rode the train into Chicago. Usually, when driving into the city, I pop in a CD of Carl Sandburg's poem "Windy City" as I approach the Chicago Skyway. The skyway is an elevated 8-mile section of highway that rises over the Calumet River south of the city. It is from here that I get my first glimpse of the Chicago skyline across the lake.

Sandburg is known for shorter works – the six-lined "Fog" (about fog and cat feet) comes to mind – but his poem about Chicago is over fifteen minutes long. The recording I have is of Carl Sandburg reading his poem. When he says the name of the windy city, he intones it: *Chicaaaooogoooo.* He sing-songs the name, pulls it like taffy. The poem chronicles the rise of the city by the lake, the building and breaking down, the people, the neighborhoods, the stockyards and steel. And the jazz.

Chicaaaooogooooo.

A large part of Chicago's appeal is that it sits on the edge of Lake Michigan. The city has gone to great lengths to preserve its relationship with the lake. The first map of Chicago drawn up in 1836 had "Public Ground – A Common to Remain Forever Open, Clear, and Free of any buildings, or Other Obstruction whatever" written along the lakefront land. This phrase set forth a precedent to preserve Chicago's shore.

The architect Daniel Burnham was a strong proponent for Chicago's lakefront. The year I began my Lake Trek was the 100th anniversary of his "Plan of Chicago." This work birthed American urban planning and is a touchstone even today. Burnham designed the city with the lakeshore acting as Chicago's front yard and open entryway to the lake.

I chose to begin the Lake Trek in Chicago for several reasons. First, it was the perfect marker as the beginning and end of the trek. I would be able to see the skyline for miles as I left the city and as I approached it at the end. Second, I could take the train into the city to begin. Third, I wanted to walk the south side of the lake first.

The southern curve of Lake Michigan is highly industrialized, riddled with immense steel mills, container ports, cement factories, and one of the nation's largest oil refineries. I wanted to walk this segment first to both get it out of the way and to be able to relate it to the rest of the lake.

When most people think of Lake Michigan, they envision the singing sands, the wide beaches, the clean waters. Robert Macfarlane said in his book *The Wild Places* that "certain landscapes might hold certain thoughts." I wanted to have sand dune and lakeshore thoughts, but in this first part of my trek I'd have to welcome steel mill and railroad thoughts, shipping canal and abandoned building thoughts. I knew I'd have to pass through the hard truth of the southern rim of the lake with its soot and sparks and industrial sounds.

The dirty silver Amtrak train scooted through the industrial corridor into the south side of Chicago. Through the streaked and cloudy window, I saw long trains of mounded coal cars, fenced yards outside of factories filled with long sheets or thick cords of coiled steel, and many, many abandoned buildings. I was familiar with this area in concept, from a distance in a fast-moving car. After walking this segment, I'd have a boots-on-the-ground, soot-in-the-lungs intimacy with it.

But, first, I had to arrive at the beginning: Chicago.

Begin at the beginning

If you've ever lived in the Midwest, then you can appreciate that first day when winter releases its icy-clawed grip on the land and people. The sun comes out, it hits 50 degrees, and everyone acts like they've had a triple dose of Zoloft.

March 15, the day I arrived in Chicago, was *that* day.

Winter had been exceptionally cold and snowy, one that had broken long-standing records. But the piles of dirty snow had magically disappeared with the warmth, and the sun, finally, was shining.

Beginning my adventure on the tip of Navy Pier would give me the perfect vantage point to look out on the lake and also back at the city of Chicago. The pier is almost 100 years old. During WWI, it was turned into a training facility for soldiers, and the towers of the Grand Ballroom were used as carrier pigeon stations. Between the wars, the pier reverted to a gathering place and hosted many exhibitions. During WWII, it became a training facility for naval pilots, and, after the war, the pier housed the newly established University of Illinois. Returning GIs nicknamed the school "Harvard on the Rocks." The pier has since evolved into the tourist spot it is today. There are restaurants, museums, a Shakespeare Theater, and amusement rides, in addition to the docking places available for boats to take locals and tourists on jaunts out on the lake.

The night before beginning the Lake Trek, a mixture of excitement and anticipation kept me awake. Would I be able to complete these first 70 miles in the five days I'd allowed myself, let alone all 1,000? After just a few hours of sleep, I woke early and hustled the several blocks to Navy Pier. As I walked the length of the deserted pier, the sun lifted itself out of the lake and balanced on its edge. The day was crisp, the wind mild, and the forecast was for it to warm into the 60s.

I was thrilled and, yes, a little – if not scared – then a bit overwhelmed at the scale of what I was about to begin. The lake surrounded me. I could look north up its length and see nothing but smooth water, and east across its width and see its flat expanse. Then, I turned south. The rim of the lake is studded for miles with boxy factories and steel mills with tall chimneys topped with smoky plumes. The breeze was from the south, so the gray and black smoke trailed out over the lake, reaching toward me like dissipating fingers. How, exactly, does one walk through all of that industry? I was about to find out if it was even possible.

After months of training and planning, I was at the beginning. From the end of the pier, I looked back at the city. This is a wonderful thing about Chicago: you can be in a park or on a pier or even the museum campus and look back at the buildings. From some angles you can even catch the city's reflection on the lake. It is gorgeous. I took in the moment, snapped some photos of me with the city, the pier, the lake in the background, I breathed in the clean lake air, and turned on my GPS unit. Then, I took the very first steps of my 1,000-Mile Walk on the Beach.

From downtown Chicago and south to Hyde Park there are lovely pathways through parks along the lakefront. I'd planned this first day to be only 10 miles. This would be a relatively easy walk that would put me in a good position for the next day.

The first few miles took me from Navy Pier to the Alder Planetarium. This U-shaped hike spanned Grant Park and provided wonderful views of the lake and the city. On a clear day, you can see Chicago from the far-off Michigan side where I would end this segment's trek – over 70 miles away by land, about half that distance when you look back over the lake. In these early miles, it was comforting to watch the buildings come alive in the morning light.

Rounding the end of the museum campus, I noticed how calm the lake was. A wide, concrete slab that tilts slightly toward the lake rims the planetarium. This walkway seemed to blend with the calm, unmoving water. Since it was still technically winter, I was lucky to get this gentle beginning to my journey.

I made my way around the empty and iced-over marina and skirted Soldier Field and McCormick Place. I curved off the path whenever a patch of beach presented itself. The walking was easy and pleasant. I passed many people using the pathway in the mild weather. Often, I glanced back at the receding skyline.

Hyde Park is home to the University of Chicago. The University has an important connection with the lake in the person of Dr. Henry Cowles who was a Professor of Botany there in the early 1900s. From his many visits to wilderness areas around Chicago, he came to understand that landscapes and habitats change and evolve, a revolutionary thought at the time. A large swath of his old stomping grounds is now protected as the Indiana Dunes National Lakeshore. That park, lying still a good number of miles ahead of me, encompasses some of the most biodiverse and unique habitats on the planet.

After dinner, I went to a small grocery store and chose some fruit. Then I saw a small container of olives and feta cheese in olive oil. Thinking

I'd go for *haute cuisine* Lake Trek snacks, I grabbed it along with some crackers. My staple snack of almond M&Ms – while delightful – could use some classing up. I settled into my room and organized my backpack while watching the news.

The lead story that night was yet another fatal shooting of a high school student on Chicago's South Side, the 28th student to be murdered in Chicago that school year. The report told how the young man had died shielding two younger kids in the back seat of a mini van.

I knew that the South Side was rough. I had lived in Detroit in the past, though, so I was familiar with rough neighborhoods. Part of taking the measure of Lake Michigan would be a commitment to experiencing the entire shoreline, not just the sandy beaches we are all drawn to.

The next morning, I began walking in time to see the sun rising behind the Museum of Science and Industry at the north end of Jackson Park. This park was the location of the World's Columbian Exposition of 1893. Daniel Burnham designed most of the buildings for the event and the Museum of Science and Industry is a permanent version of one of his buildings. Frederick Law Olmstead designed the park. He's the same landscape designer who created Manhattan's Central Park, Brooklyn's Prospect Park, and the grounds around the U.S. Capitol Building, among many other prominent projects.

I wandered over several small bridges and greeted a gentleman casting the first fishing line of the day into the still waters there. Then I came upon a formal Japanese garden. An arched wooden bridge lifted me over a stream. I walked through stones arranged to catch the morning light. I had just started the day and was eager to put some miles behind me, but it was so tranquil that I sat and spent a few slow, beautiful minutes watching the sun lift itself fully from the lake.

A great place to dump a body

Jackson Park transitioned into the large expanse of land around the South Shore Country Club and, after several blocks of neighborhoods, into Rainbow Park. This park butts up against the former site of U.S. Steel's South Works mill. This is where the steel was forged to build the John Hancock Center and Sears Tower. The mill operated for over 100 years, closing for good in the 1990s. At its height, 20,000 people worked there. Iron and water go together because Lake Michigan provides a way for vast quantities of iron ore and limestone to be shipped to the mill.

Now, every trace of the South Works mill has been scoured from the land. All that remains are hundreds of acres of feral, trash-strewn scrubland. While there are optimistic plans to develop the site with housing and retail, parks and a marina, it stands as a post-industrial, polluted scar on the lakeshore.

The night before, I had set out some rules to keep myself safe for the rest of this segment:

1. Don't walk through areas that look like a good place to dump a body.
2. Don't take photos where people might get angry about someone taking photos.
3. Don't take photos near any place that looks like a meth house.
4. Start early in the morning, and end well before dusk.

I walk on the fractured sidewalk near the fence, trying to pick my way through all the trash and broken glass. There isn't a single footstep where I don't crunch glass shards beneath my boots. The fence is so close that I can reach out my left hand and touch it. A tall berm of dirt on the other side of the fence prevents me from seeing the steel mill site. Between the dirt and the fence are piles of trash: smashed bottles and dirty diapers, fast-food wrappers and plastic bags darting in the breeze. I want to get a good photo of the site, but it is not the kind of neighborhood where one climbs barbed wire-topped fences.

Across the narrow street a row of beaten, small houses squat close together. A large man stands on his slanting front porch watching me pass. He clenches and unclenches his massive hands as he tracks me with his eyes; is he angry at something? A street-sweeper machine races up the road. Who knew they could move so fast? It doesn't clean the street, it just races through the torn-up neighborhood. On the next block is an enormous church with a spire reaching for the clouds, a monument to the wealth and community that once was here. The area around the fenced church is broken and mostly abandoned.

I walk quickly and catch up to two elementary school-aged brothers with backpacks. As I pass them, they look up at me like I'm an apparition.

I smile and say, "Good Morning!"

They look at me, then at each other, then back again. The smaller one asks his brother, "What did she say?"

I keep smiling and say, "Hello!" but they seem befuddled by what this is all about. I keep walking, and they fall far behind.

Tiny, tired houses now crowd the sidewalk; their porches almost touch it. Every so often, a house is missing on the street, the place where it stood now a gouged-out hole where useless things are tossed. Often, the houses on either side are scorched and blackened; sometimes siding is warped from the heat of the fire that consumed the house now absent. There are many sites that look like a good place to dump a body or like a meth house.

Or, seriously, both.

In Detroit, I lived near Mexican Village, a neighborhood that had a bakery that made wonderful pastries. As I walk south on Commercial Avenue past all the gated stores and restaurants, I smell something that takes me back to that Detroit neighborhood. Across the street, I see a Mexican bakery called Marzeya.

When I enter the place, I gasp. The perimeter of the space is lined with cases filled with tray after tray of elaborate pastries. I wander from one to the next, studying the flaky creations through the glass doors. Behind the counter, 50-pound bags of flour are stacked five high. Through a small window, I see the white-aproned workers in the back, kneading dough and tending the large ovens.

I circle the cases listening to customers converse in rapid Spanish as they pay for their pastries. There is comfort in this warm, safe space which smells of butter and flour after walking for miles exposed and vulnerable on the street. I'd like to linger here, but there are no tables or chairs. I take my time, eventually choosing two large pastries. One is filled with cream cheese, the other is a massive apple turnover. I take them to the woman behind the counter. She has been studying me – my backpack, my boots – and I know I don't fit here. Part of me wants to explain what I'm doing, but I can't find the words. I realize that I haven't had a conversation with anyone since leaving home. Even though that was only three days ago, it feels like a month, and I the only thing I can think to say to this woman is *gracias.*

There's something about eating when you're hungry from walking a long way. It is more elemental and satisfying. I savor that first pastry. It is light and layered and buttery, and the cream cheese filling seems to be whipped up with kindness and sweetness. I tuck the second pastry inside my sling pack with my other snacks, the M&Ms and small container of olives and feta cheese.

I head due east on 92nd Street toward the lake and to one of the few bridges over the Calumet River that cuts through the South Works site. One of the reasons that Chicago can be a shining city on the lake is because of the Calumet. This was an alternative shipping and industrial corridor so that the Chicago River didn't have to always play that role.

Welcome to Indiana!

I hustled out of Calumet Park and alongside the Chicago Skyway, the elevated superhighway that soars over this neighborhood. I'd seen the view many times while driving on its elevated surface, but now, down at lake level, I looked up at the structure while traffic and exhaust enveloped me.

For part of the way, there was a paved bike/pedestrian path running between the skyway and U.S. Highway 12/20. Walking there was like being the meat in a vehicle sandwich, but at least there was a path.

Soon, I saw the "Welcome to Indiana" sign. It was here that I said farewell to paved pathways. Stepping off the hard surface, I began walking on the side of the road in the winter-dead, knee-high, trash-strewn weeds.

Welcome to Indiana, indeed.

I'd driven this way countless times – crossed from my home state of Michigan, through Indiana, and into Illinois. This time, though, under my own power, I had walked from one state into another, and would cross the next border into Michigan before this segment was complete.

The day was predicted to hit the 70s. I hiked along US 12/20, past railroad yards and lots where weeds struggled to envelope abandoned vehicles and rusting machinery, past the seven-story tall glittering sign for the Horseshoe Casino, and into the city of Whiting. Though hemmed in by industry and expressways, this little town was surprisingly tranquil. I walked to Whiting's Lakefront Park where I sat and lifted my tired feet onto the bench.

I pulled the second pastry from my pack. The white bag looked like it was soaked with grease, probably the butter from inside working its way out. The next thing I pulled out was my bag of almond M&Ms, which was also dripping with oil. The pack of olives and feta had exploded, and the pungent oil soaked all of my snacks. Nothing was salvageable, and by the time I realized this, I had olive oil all over my hands.

I tossed the entire mess into a nearby trashcan, wiped my hands on some dead grass, and collapsed on the bench. My feet throbbed, I was hot and sweaty, and now all of my snacks were ruined. I looked up at the blue sky and listened to the waves murmuring. Being here, I thought, was where I had chosen to be. *Haute cuisine* snacks – while delightful – were not necessary.

I stopped feeling sorry for myself. I looked across the water to the southeast and the industry that I still had to pass through. There were steel mills and, directly south, the massive BP oil refinery that sprawled over 1,400 acres. US 12/20 bisected the installation, so I knew I could hike through the center of the complex.

Through the center of the beast ("You can't get there from here. . . .")

The forecast had been right. It was unseasonably warm for March and I hiked in a thin T-shirt and pants. Sweat soaked my back underneath my sling pack and under the single, wide strap that cut diagonally across my chest.

At one point I passed a steel-processing facility. High voltage lines looped over the road to a substation on the side of the building. There was a continuous, ominous, force-field-like hum from the massive current surging overhead. The hair on the top of my head lifted as I passed.

This area was not designed for foot traffic, so there were few sidewalks. The one stretch that I did find had hawthorn trees planted nearby so that the branches with their three-inch thorns reached for my bare arms. Between the curbs and fences was a strip of hard ground, strewn with pointy rocks and shards of rusted metal. It seemed like someone had thought about what would be the most uncomfortable substances to walk on, then filled the roadside with that.

Along the BP Refinery corridor, I took some photos with my cell phone: the black pipes curving into each other, then thrusting upward and capped with smoke or blue flames, the line of black tanker train cars behind a sooty wall, gleaming white storage tanks all in a row with power lines looping between. A BP security truck approached and slowed to my pace. I held my phone like I was talking on it, but the truck continued to tail me. Since I hadn't allowed time to be arrested, I put my phone away and waved to the driver. The truck sped away.

After finally emerging from the refinery, I approached the drawbridge passing over the Indiana Harbor Canal that separates BP's facility from the Ispat Inland Steel Mill on the lake. Tucked onto the far side of the mill's land was the casino hotel where I would stay the night, mashed between two steel mills and surrounded by a tangle of highways. I guess it was the perfect spot for a casino since they could float a boat in a walled-off lagoon there for the gambling operation.

I was fortunate that there was any place to stay along this stretch. I hadn't passed any other hotels or motels all day, not even the scary kind that rented rooms by the hour.

The bridge tender was standing outside his booth, talking on a cell phone. He glanced at me as I approached, then he rubbed his eyes and looked away, shaking his head like he was seeing things. As I began walking the incline of the bridge, I waved. He jumped. Then, apparently assured I was real, waved back. I caught sight of the lake again, which had been hidden for too long, from the middle of the bridge, and a cooling breeze caused me to linger.

From my maps, I knew that I had to pass under Highway 912, take a left, then pass under the highway again to get to the hotel on the lake. As I came off the drawbridge, I felt a large blister on my right foot explode. I hadn't even known it existed until that moment, and was glad I was within sight of my hotel. I passed under the highway, then headed toward the second underpass that did not, in fact, exist. There were only on and off ramps, and no way to get to the other side. After crossing over two of these ramps, I realized I might have to call a cab to drive me to the hotel I could so clearly see.

I could not get there from here, at least not on foot.

As I made my way down an embankment, thrashing through the thigh-high dead weeds and trash, a man in a yellow Jeep pulled over on the ramp and called to me. I told him where I needed to go and he offered a ride.

Now, I'm not one to jump into a car with a stranger, but this guy didn't look like he was looking for a place to dump a body (though I could have suggested many nearby locations).

He moved his large lunch box into the backseat and waited until I had buckled up before pulling back on the road. He had just gotten off his shift at the steel mill. Hanging from his rear view mirror was a yellow-feathered icon. I asked about it, and he told me that he got it on his recent vacation to Hawaii and that it warded off bad luck. He regaled me with some highlights from the Pacific islands while we drove the last bit of the way to my hotel. Envisioning those tropical beaches was a rather surreal way to end a day of walking through the industrial horrorscape between Chicago's South Side and Gary, Indiana. I was ever so grateful for the brief mental vacation, and for the timely ride.

Gatorade or margarita with salt?

After hiking that strange March day with its summer temperatures, I was sweaty and exhausted. I dropped my pack in the room and limped into the bathroom where I discovered a deep bathtub. I ran the bath water and dumped a small shampoo bottle in the rushing water to make a bubble bath.

When I took off my pants, I noticed that my socks were sooty, and my legs above my socks were brown with gritty grime up to the top of my knees. I'd never heard of getting grimy even underneath clothing. I washed my face, then swiped inside my ear with the washcloth. It came away black. In the tub, I soaked and soaped and scrubbed. After seeing the grimy ring in the draining tub, I took a shower to blast the last of the industrial soot off of me.

I dressed my blisters and noticed that a blister was forming underneath one of my toenails. That was new! I hobbled through the lobby to the restaurant. There were signs pointing to the casino boat, and a few portly senior citizens waddled that way. I was just happy to be able to reach the restaurant. As I sat in the booth, I thought about the hot day and how I should get a Gatorade to replace the electrolytes I'd lost.

Then, I opened the menu.

When one is faced with a decision between a sports drink and a margarita with salt, always choose the margarita. You get your sodium and chloride, plus the pain-fighting properties of tequila.

One nice thing about casino hotels: they usually have a decent restaurant. After a lamb chop dinner and lovely margarita, I stood up slowly, grimacing. By this point in the trek, anytime I sat down, the muscles in my legs and back would seize, and I'd have to struggle to stand and loosen things up before being able to hobble along again. I guess my training hadn't been hard enough to prepare me for the real thing. I limped back to my room.

I stretched out on the hotel bed and pulled out my maps to study the next day's hike. For tomorrow, it looked like the only way to get from where I was into the city of Gary would be to walk through a large train yard encircled with wetlands.

Before setting out the next day, I walked the length of Jeorse Park, a curve of rocky beach that stretched east from the hotel up to another steel mill and massive train yard. Along the way, I looked for a way to scamper over the maze of tracks, between the coal cars, through the wetlands, under the highway and into Gary. Some path that was not evident on my maps. I had no luck. I relented and walked the mile back to the hotel to call a cab to get me past all of these obstacles.

Gary, Indiana! Gary, Indiana!

I asked the cab driver to drop me at the newspaper office for Gary's *Post-Tribune*. On the short ride, the cabbie seemed to doze off several times. I tried to make conversation to keep him awake, but the man seemed too depressed, drugged, or sleepy to keep up his end, so I leaned back and watched his eyelids flutter.

We passed the two-story, brick Post-Tribune building with all the windows covered with brown paper. We continued up the street and he dropped me at a strip mall where the tiny newspaper office was smashed between two failing businesses. There was an intercom, but the door opened without having to be buzzed in. Two elderly women customers startled when they saw me enter. Even the newspaper lady, safe behind thick Plexiglas, looked scared.

I had heard things about Gary. I knew that it had the distinction of being the murder capital of the U.S. for a couple years. I'd driven through it a couple of times when diverted from the highway during construction and knew Gary was a rough place. But how mean does a city have to be to have its newspaper office turned into a panic room?

I remembered a time in the 1980s when I was living in Detroit. I went to the local chain grocery store (before it left the city for good), and told the cashier that I needed to get some film for my camera. She nodded and said, "Oh, it's over by checkout one. But hold on a sec." She turned toward the cashier at that station and shouted, "Lois! She's coming over, but it's okay! She needs film! She is UNARMED!" Poor Lois froze anyway and stared at me like I was going to shoot her. I lifted my hands to prove that I was, indeed, unarmed, then slowly went over, hands raised the entire time, to get my film.

That's how mean Detroit was back then.

"Hi," I said through the Plexiglas to the skittish woman on the other side. "My name is Loreen, and I'm walking all the way around Lake Michigan." I placed a card with my information about the Lake Trek into the stainless steel tray and the woman lifted it out on the other side. "In case your paper is interested in the story."

"The main office isn't here anymore," she said. "It's in Merrillville."

"Where's that?" I asked, thinking I could walk there if it was along the way.

"Ten miles south."

"Okay. I'm on foot."

She stared at me.

"I'm walking around the lake right now."

Again, a blank stare.

"Could you at least send my card to the main office?"

Something clicked with her. She almost smiled. "Okay, I'll send this to the main office." She tossed the card into a lone plastic bin against the wall. The rest of the narrow office had only one, mostly empty desk.

Stepping back outside, I began walking Gary's main road toward US 12. Along the way, I noticed how broken the city was, how fractured the community, how beaten the few people I passed appeared. As I walked toward the lake, I noticed a distant thrumming that grew in intensity until it was a physical presence I was moving against.

That sound, that force, was United States Steel Gary Works.

When this complex was built, it was the largest steel mill in the world.

The town of Gary was constructed in 1901 by J.P. Morgan and Elbert H. Gary to house the workers for the mill. It was, and still is, the largest "company town" ever built in America. Twelve thousand acres of dunes were leveled, and a giant workforce flocked to Gary from all sectors of America along with many European immigrants. It was a living community, much like the Southside of Chicago, until the 1980s when the steel jobs began to disappear.

Once, Gary was called things like: "The Magic City of Steel," and "The City of the Century," and an "Industrial Utopia." Gary even had its own song, "Garyland, My Garyland," sung at the celebration to welcome the very first iron ore boat on July 23, 1908:

> *The wheels of progress all will hum;*
> *And Gary will be going some,*
> *Through all the splendid years to come,*
> *Garyland, my Garyland.*

U.S. Highway 12, my nemesis

In the center of downtown Gary is a sculpture to honor the steel mill. It is a larger-than-life depiction of several men in protective, reflective heat suits, gloved and masked and helmeted, staring into a caldron of molten steel. Flames dance around them. It is fantastic.

I took some photos, and then booked out of there. By this time, U.S. Highway 12 had become my nemesis. It allowed me to skirt much of the industry in this area, but I wanted to be on the lakeshore.

US 12 is one of the oldest highways in the nation, running from downtown Detroit all the way to the Pacific coast. Though most of the heavy traffic now rides on superhighways I-94 and I-90, US 12 is still an important local road. It passes through some post-apocalyptic areas with boarded-up buildings named "Pandora's" – a strip club – and "Dom and Peter's Point View Bar" strung out along the empty lots where mutant plants struggle through cracked concrete.

From the east side of Gary, I had about four miles to go before I could get off the road, turn north, and finally hit the beach again. When I got beyond the last overpass outside of Gary, water-filled ditches paralleled the road and the sound of croaking frogs competed with the throbbing pulse of the mill receding behind me. Nature persists in the oddest places. In a triangle of land between an on and off ramp to US 12, a pair of killdeer were calling to each other.

Now, I understand the frogs being there. You hatch, you're a tadpole, then a frog in a ditch. But birds? They migrate, they fly! They had seen nicer options than the side of US 12! At least that what I would have thought were I a bird and could spread my wings to lift me to a more gentle place.

I soon hit a little pocket of civilization near the Miller station on the electric-powered interurban South Shore Line. Turning north, I headed toward my first stretch of the Indiana Dunes National Lakeshore: Marquette Beach. I longed to get out to the lake, to see real Lake Michigan sand, and to get away from the industry and trash.

When I noticed sand drifting out of a scrubby lawn, and then looked up and saw the lake, I couldn't stop smiling. I wished that it was warm enough to plunge into the water to wash the grip and grime of Gary off of me, but it was chilly and windy. I made do with the sound of the waves replacing the sounds of the mill, with the fresh wind blowing from across hundreds of miles of the lake, to the feel of soft sand under my boots instead of rubble and trash and weeds.

Taking flight

I started to run.

Even though I was tired and the blisters on my feet were blistering yet again, I ran. Arms extended, I frightened a group of gulls at the water's edge, and they took flight as I glided by.

Okay, I didn't run for long. But it was exhilarating while it lasted. I had the beach to myself. I stood just out of the reach of the waves and looked north up the 300 miles of the lake, over the expanse of water. From the curve of the lakeshore, I figured I was at the southernmost point of Lake Michigan. Two steel mills bookended the beach. The juxtaposition of wild nature and man's attempt to melt, cast, and control it disturbed me.

When I reached Portage's steel mill, I made my way to my hotel and a pocket of commerce that promised a good cup of coffee and a steak dinner. And even, I would soon learn, a pomegranate margarita.

By this point in the trek, I had gotten pretty comfortable handing people my promotional postcard, and saying, "That's me" (in the picture), "I'm walking around Lake Michigan!" Most everyone thought it was a great idea and had many questions: Where do you stay? How far do you walk each day? How do you know which way to go?

And: Did you walk through Gary? Are you crazy?

At this hotel, I gave the postcard to the young woman at the check-in and thanked her for having a room for me. The next morning, as I was checking out, a different woman kept looking at me, then at something next to her computer. She pulled out my postcard. "I thought it was you!" She thought the Lake Trek was a fantastic idea.

Industrial legacy lives on

I had to get around yet another steel mill, a large cement factory, and the Port of Indiana before heading back to the lake. By the time I'd passed these last industrialized sections, I began to understand the immensity of scale on which man had contorted the lower rim of the lake. The steel mill in Gary, the oil refinery in Whiting, and the cement factory in Bluffington Harbor were the world's largest when built. Industrial tycoons like J. P. Morgan and J.D. Rockefeller dreamed big in this era of industrialization, and their legacy is still mostly intact here.

In the case of BP's Whiting refinery, it's actually expanding with the facility undergoing a $4 billion expansion as I walked through it.

The lake's edge was the logical location for these facilities, especially the southern edge with its canals and waterways connecting the lake to America's heartland and the Mississippi River. It made sense to locate industries which needed to bring in large quantities of raw products by water and rail, to locate ports that could handle both river barges and lake-going vessels, to build massive cement factories to use the mountains of slag cast-off by the steel mills, to build refineries to crack molecules of heavy crude into light gasoline for our cars.

It made sense for industry to settle here, but the lake has suffered because of it. If after walking one day through this area I was covered in soot and grime, how much has the lake absorbed over the last century?

The BP refinery processes over 400,000 barrels of crude oil *per day*. It is currently completely legal for the refinery to dump approximately 1,500 pounds of ammonia and 5,000 pounds of toxic sludge *per day* into

Lake Michigan. With the expansion of the facility, the company wants to increase this. To get around the Clean Water Act, the company has been allowed to pre-dilute what it dumps – to draw water from farther out in the lake, dilute the waste, then dump it offshore.

The problem of supplying our country with gasoline is complex, but the lake is suffering.

Dunes for canning jars

The next morning was cold. I put on most of my layers along with gloves before heading out. The cold numbed much of the pain in my feet and legs, though I started the day with muscle knots along the sides of my shins. I didn't even know it was possible to get knots there. I hadn't prepared my feet for the beating they were taking, and hadn't brought along socks for both 70 degree and freezing temperatures.

In the community of Dune Acres, I met a retired man who had worked for over 30 years at the Gary steel mill. His job was in the coalhouse, where they slit the large rolls of steel to size for different industries.

"Whirlpool might order it this wide," he spread his hands about a yard apart, "for their fridges," he said. "Car companies might want it wider for mini-van hoods. We'd slit the rolls of steel to order, roll it back up, and ship it out. Thirty years I slit steel."

"Did you live in Gary?" I asked.

He smiled. "Yeah. First twelve years or so. Three or four of us guys would share a house. We had some good times. Gary had a lot going on then. Good restaurants, a nice movie theater. Then things went downhill."

"What happened? It looked like a bomb went off."

He shook his head and muttered about corrupt government, the influx of drugs, the loss of jobs, but he couldn't fully explain its downfall. The smile left his face and he looked at his boots.

"Dune Acres seems nice," I offered.

He inhaled sharply. "Yep. The wife and I like it here."

After saying goodbye to him, I walked out to the lake on the curvy, neighborhood roads. From this point to Michigan City was over seven miles of expansive beach.

The day got progressively windier, so I wound my scarf around my head. I followed a deer path back into the low fore-dunes to take a break.

There, I nestled on a spot bare of dune grass.

Out of the wind, it was almost pleasant in the sun. I reclined and looked up at the crystalline, blue sky. Pulling out my cell phone, I called my sister, Leslie.

"Hey, Lake Trekker! Where are you?"

My voice caught in my throat at the sound of her familiar voice. "Hi. Almost to Michigan City," I finally answered. "Nothing but beach ahead of me."

"Yaaay! So I can stop worrying?" We laughed. We didn't chat too long since I didn't want my muscles to cool down and lock up. As I told her about some of the tougher stretches, I allowed the realization to wash over me that the most industrialized part of my adventure was finally behind me. Soon, I was up and walking again.

Farther up the beach, a leopard frog sat at the edge of the waves. It wasn't quite dead, but it had that *I must have come out of hibernation too soon* look on its face. I thought of trying to warm him in my hands, but knew the day would never warm to the point of keeping him alive. I wondered if hypothermia affected amphibians the same way it does humans. Do they, too, want to strip off all their clothes because their befuddled brain suddenly tells them they are too hot? Did this frog think he was actually baking in the sun?

As I approached Michigan City, the dunes started to rise along the shoreline. I headed inland between two tall dunes. A couple of years back, I had climbed the largest one here, Mt. Baldy. It is over 100 feet tall and is a living dune. That is, it moves. It migrates about 5 feet a year, swallowing anything in its path.

It may not sound like such a great feat to climb a dune of this height, but it is so steep that for every five steps up, you slide back four. The view from the top is spectacular. On a clear day you can see a suggestion of the Chicago skyline across 35 miles of blue lake.

Clearly in view from the top of Mt. Baldy, nestled down in the dunes, is a maximum-security state penitentiary. This would be my idea of cruel and unusual punishment: incarceration near enough to the lake to catch a cooling breeze, but never able to see the water or walk the shore.

I looked across the distance of the lake and, sure enough, could pick out the toy-like forms of the tallest buildings in Chicago. I swept my eyes along the miles I had traveled, past the clusters of billowing smokestacks on the rim of the lake. The miles had been more difficult than I had imagined, the industry entangled in a web of railroad tracks, the lakeshore obscured, reshaped and deformed for much of the way. I was glad that I had walked this stretch at the very beginning, thankful that it was now behind me.

The park I was now walking was established in the 1960s as the Indiana Dunes National Lakeshore. Prior to that, industry made use of the sand there. There was once a dune, now gone, almost twice the height of Mt. Baldy. It was called Hoosier Slide. If you have a very old Ball canning jar, it's quite possible that it was made with sand from Hoosier Slide because the entire dune was melted down to make them.

The Indiana Dunes National Lakeshore set aside 18 miles of shoreline and over 14,000 acres of dunes, beach, marsh, and forest. Some ecosystems here are unique to the planet. I saw tracks of deer and raccoon and saw large flocks of migrating ducks. I also saw my first ladybug of the year on this stretch of shoreline. It had that same *I hatched a little too early* look on its face (if you looked really, really close).

The wind died down as I walked between the dunes and away from the lake onto a street that would lead me, once again, to US 12. I walked the shoulder of my nemesis until I was able to turn off on a side street into the heart of Michigan City, Indiana, and toward where I would stay the night.

The historic Feallock House B&B didn't take credit cards, I was advised when I made the reservation, so could I please send a check? I had done so, and included a quick note about my Lake Trek. Janet (owner, chef, greeter, and housekeeper of the place) had known about my adventure before I arrived – limping on my blistered feet and bundled against the cold and below-freezing wind chill – on her wooden front porch. She still seemed surprised to see me.

The Puppet Master

"When I first saw you, I thought you were the handyman," she says, finally ushering me in. I put my pack down and uncoil the orange scarf from around my neck and open my wool vest. I haven't looked in the mirror for a while, but now think that I probably look pretty strange with all my layers.

Janet scurries ahead of me, giving me a quick tour of the place. I limp along gamely. She introduces Charlie, her dog, before we head upstairs. I choose the bedroom closest to the deep, claw-foot tub. She rushes around the room, showing me how to work the electric fireplace, the shades, and the storage for the extra blankets. At this point, my head is spinning because I am finally warming up.

"I'll leave you to get settled, then." And she's gone. After exploding my pack on the bed, I soak in that tub.

After I am warm and relaxed, I hobble back downstairs where Janet shares her dinner of soup and bread. She asks me about my Lake Trek, but I'm so exhausted I'm barely able to string a few sentences together. She tells me much about the history and current events of Michigan City. Then, she rapidly explains the plan for the next day. She has invited several prominent people from the community to breakfast with me. She called the newspaper and had left a message at the Mayor's office.

Now, I am a little delirious from walking almost 20 miles in the freezing cold that day, then soaking in a hot tub, and I think I'm hearing things. Janet speaks quickly, like a drill sergeant, and there is really no way to process all of it in my exhausted, over-relaxed, and still-in-pain state, so I just nod a lot and hope it will sort itself out after a good night's sleep.

I mean, seriously, the Mayor?

Breakfast was at 8:30, so after a superb night's sleep I got ready, and descended the stairs limping a little, but with much refreshed legs. I walked through the downstairs trying to piece together what was real and what was hallucination from the night before. The dining room was set for eight with formal, lake-themed china, so I figured some people really would be joining me for breakfast. I found Janet in the kitchen and she shooed me over to the coffee. Soon, the head of the Main Street Association and his wife arrived, then a local artist and his wife. We chatted until Janet herded us all to the food she had set out on the antique buffet.

These were lovely people, concerned about and involved with their community, happy to meet me, and I them. We ate a wonderful breakfast together. Janet called me from the table to talk to the reporter on the phone. When I was done, Janet informed me that the Mayor was in meetings all morning, but a City Councilman would see me off at the beach along with the reporter I had just spoken with. I was in awe.

"You are a *Puppet Master*, Janet!" I told her, and we laughed together. Her laugh, I thought, was just a little diabolical.

At Janet's bidding, the reporter, the artist's wife, the City Councilman and his little daughter saw me off at the Michigan City Beach. I waved good-bye to the gathering and jogged up the beach and into the sunny last day of this segment. When I slowed to a walk, I looked back and watched their cars file out of the beach parking lot, leaving it completely empty.

I was alone again with the lake.

The morning breeze was mild and the temperature in the mid-20s when I left Michigan City and set off on a northeasterly heading. The shore began to curve back up toward the state of Michigan.

The sand is fine, almost white. Here, the beach truly "sings." This phenomenon happens when you scuff your feet along, or, if the wind is just right, the sand particles will give off a tone or hum as they are blown across each other. It only happens if the grains of sand are the right size and a certain silica composition, and if the humidity is within a certain range.

It happens there.

I only passed one other person that morning, a woman who was picking up trash on the beach. Understand that most of the trash on a beach like this comes from the lake, not from the people on the shore. Things fall off boats in the summer, or someone in Wisconsin dumps medical waste into the lake, or major lake cities expel sewage into the lake when their water-treatment facilities are overwhelmed during heavy rains (which happens all the time). That trash is slowly distributed onto the shoreline, mostly on the east side due to the prevailing winds.

I had walked by chunks of boats, Styrofoam coolers, and half-drunk bottles of orange pop. Some of the stranger pieces of trash were a cracked coconut still full of white meat, a dried gourd, and lots of colorful ribbons, often tangled up in zebra mussel shells (from zebra mussel birthday parties?).

This woman combing the beach lived on the stretch near the state line. I asked her if I was in Michigan yet. She pointed out the blue house on the border.

I told her that I had walked from Chicago and now, five days later, was here.

She asked, "Don't you ever get lonely?"

"No," I answered, "I have The Lake!"

She nodded and smiled like she understood. Or maybe she thought I

33

was crazy and should humor me. I believe she had a love of the lake since she was picking up bits of trash and detritus from zebra mussel parties.

A rocky end to the segment

As I got closer to the city of New Buffalo and could see the jetty from the harbor, I came across piles of rocks placed to stop the erosion of the hills abutting the lake. I climbed over the first stretch of these, careful to avoid the ice still forming from the spray of the waves, but soon I came across a pumping station rimmed with dangerously icy rocks. I went inland and approached New Buffalo from the streets.

I stopped in at the local newspaper office and tried to speak to the clerk there. I hadn't realized that my mouth was numb from the freezing weather. When I wrote my cell number down for her to give to a reporter, I noticed that my hand was shaking. I guessed that climbing on those icy rocks had taken more out of me than I had thought. Or maybe it was the almost 70 miles I had walked in the heat and the cold over the last five days.

After walking another 4 miles, the restaurant that was my destination for this first leg of my journey, my pick-up point, finally appeared. My mom and brother were going to meet me there to take me home to Battle Creek, for a few days rest.

I unwound the scarf from my head and tried to take a picture of the smile frozen on my face with a sign for the Red Arrow Roadhouse in the background.

I limped inside the roadhouse on swollen and blistered feet, amazed at what I'd accomplished. But looking ahead, I wondered what in the hell I'd gotten myself into.

Segment 2

March 24–26
Union Pier to South Haven, MI
with Ben
53 miles in 3 days

Total Trek Mileage: 125 miles

A sane person would have. . .

. . . taken a couple of weeks off. Maybe would have gone to the doctor about the condition of her feet.

Maybe would have stopped to reconsider the whole undertaking.

But I had told Ben and Lucas that they would be joining me on short segments of the Lake Trek during their spring breaks, and Ben was on deck for the coming leg of the walk. I had planned to walk the majority of this adventure alone, but I realized it was also a special opportunity to share some time with my sons.

Ben's break from Calvin College began immediately after I finished the first segment, so I had only three days off before we headed back to the lakeshore. Those few days at home were spent elevating and icing my swollen and battered feet and watching with fascination as one of my toenails popped off.

There was a wizened look on Jim's face when he passed me sprawled on the couch.

Was it in my imagination that it seemed to say, "See? Was that really *necessary?*"

I just sneered at the pain and gave him a "Don't you dare say it!" look. And took more Advil.

Dangerous waters

For the past ten years, I'd often instigated family trips to the lake. For several of those vacations, we'd booked rental homes for a week in the summer. These homes were along this next stretch of shoreline.

These times were shared with friends and family as everyone would meet up at our big rental house. My sister Leslie and her husband, my cousin Milene and her family, my mom and brother Phil, my friend Robin and her family would pop out to join us for part of the week. We'd cram into the house each night to cook big meals and play games with the kids, then spill out onto the beach during the sunny, summer days.

There was one year I remember when I drove with Ben and Lucas to the lake house; Jim was driving up separately a little later. All the way there, I had Sheryl Crow's song, "Soak Up the Sun," blasting on the car stereo, on repeat. I sang at the top of my lungs, the windows were rolled down so the wind could stream through the car. My boys sang along a time or two, then just stared out at the scenery, letting the song and the breeze rush over them.

The Lake has always meant freedom to me, a loosening of life, a celebration, a relaxed time to reconnect to those who are closest to me. And to reconnect to Lake Michigan. There is a magnetic pull the lake exerts on me and a "clicking in" that happens when I step foot on the lakeshore.

I have heard stories about how the monarch butterflies gather in the fall at the north end of the lake. How they rest together for a couple of days before beginning their migration to Mexico. How they fly in a long, orange-and-black cloud south over the lake until they reach a certain spot.

Then, the butterflies make a ninety-degree turn. They make that turn where there are no markers of any kind. Something in the lake tells them to turn. They do it every year at the same spot. Scientists have not been able to explain why.

There is something in the lake that draws me back, that pulls on me, directs me like that cloud of butterflies. Part of the reason for my adventure was to explore this connection in a prolonged way so that I could understand and, maybe, articulate it.

One of the favorite activities of the kids while at the lake house was to walk the beach until they found a stream. They'd meticulously dam it up with sand and rocks, let the water build up, then loosen the stones and watch the water rush to merge with the lake. They'd do it over and over again until an adult finally herded them back to the house.

On a return hike from one of these beach streams on a gorgeous July day in 2003, I remember that the four kids with me asked if they could swim back instead of walking. The lake was calm with mild waves. I told them it was okay, as long as they were on the near sandbar. I walked parallel with them on the beach. I told Ben, the oldest, to keep close to Sammy, the youngest. And I motioned to Lucas and Sheridan that they were to swim close to each other.

The kids did not know – but I did – that a few weeks earlier, six people had been swept out into the lake and drowned from this very stretch of beach. A storm had blown the day before that terrible event, causing a *seiche* or "standing wave," pushing the water up the beaches on the Michigan side. When the wind died down, all that water slowly sloshed back causing vicious riptides where sandbars broke open.

Think of an industrial fan blowing down on a kid's swimming pool. When you turn off the fan, the water that had been pushed up against the far side rushes back to find its equilibrium. One of the victims, I heard, was fifteen and a strong swimmer. I had heard that people died trying to save others.

But I had been in the lake earlier that morning and there was no rip tide. So I let the kids wade out to the sand bar. And I kept a careful eye on them as I walked, watching for any signs that they were tiring.

As is custom on the beach, I always greet walkers going the opposite direction, so I lifted a hand to a fit, middle-aged man in passing. He was watching the kids, too, but he looked pained.

"Please," he whispered, "call them in."

"Pardon?" I said.

"Call them in. Do you know what happened here last month?" He looked strong, tanned and toned, wearing only his swimming trunks, but his knees looked as though they might buckle beneath him. "Please," he repeated.

I called the kids in – to much groaning and complaining – to take the pain from the man's eyes, but he only watched until they were safe in knee-deep water before he lowered his eyes and continued walking.

When I read more about the deaths later, I found out that a middle-aged couple had drowned at Cherry Beach near where we were walking. I wondered if he knew them.

We are drawn to water. It certainly gives life, is vital for life to continue, but it can also take it. We can all hum the song "The Edmund Fitzgerald" about the sinking of that freighter in Lake Superior. It's a sad song, but it is accepted that anyone who works on a large body of water has a compact with the vast liquid around them. They realize that there is a chance, however small, that they may one day end up at the bottom of the lake.

But kids on a beach don't have this compact. Fifteen-year-olds jumping around in the waves have no such understanding. That middle-aged couple swimming together probably had no expectation that something so pleasurable could be so dangerous in certain conditions.

Down to the beach

My brother, Phil, drove Ben and me out to Cherry Beach for the beginning of Segment 2. Descending a series of steps, we dropped down the wooded bluff to the wide, sandy beach.

Ben confessed to being excited about joining me on the Lake Trek. For my part, I always get happy when first seeing the lake after any absence, so I was giggling and jumping around, albeit gingerly, on my sore feet. Ben tied a black bandana around his wild mane of auburn hair, and we set off up the beach on a northeasterly path.

Soon we reached Warren Dunes State Park. As we passed through, the park was completely empty except for two people climbing the massive dunes in the distance. It was strange to see it so quiet and serene, with huge expanses of sand scoured clean of all the summer footprints by the winter winds.

Ben had just turned 19. He's studying to be an engineer and is a sweet kid with a great sense of humor. I was looking forward to sharing this time with him, to talking about things that matter. We did talk about those things that first day: school, his friends, his classes, his hopes and dreams, was he happy? Something about that movement on the beach, the singing sands humming beneath our feet, gave a timeless quality – or maybe removed from time – and gave us space to talk.

Ben began hopping along a ridge in the sand, a side-to-side kind of happy dance.

"It's good to see you so happy," I said.

"I am happy."

"Do you feel at home at college?" He nodded. "Then it's a good fit for you. I know you've made a lot of good friends."

"I have. That's the best part."

"And the worst?"

"I don't feel challenged in my classes yet. I'm not sure I ever will there."

Ben has one of those minds that grasp everything fully the first time he hears it; he can usually think his way through tests without studying. As we walked along, we talked about taking higher-level courses, auditing classes, and looking ahead to grad school. Then, I brought up his girlfriend.

"How is it being in a relationship?"

He smiled. "I like it."

"What's the best thing?"

"I think just knowing that I'm one of the most important people in her life. Like she is to me."

It's scary to send a kid off to college, then to see how they've changed during that first year. Ben seemed to be more "Ben" than before, comfortable in his own skin, even more confident and at ease. He had grown as a person while away, and I was delighted to get to know him on a deeper level as we walked.

Nukes on the beach

If you've ever traveled I-94 north of the town of Union Pier, you've probably noticed the long line of car-sized, white granite blocks along the west side of the freeway. It stretches for miles, looking like a Christo-meets-Andy-Goldsworthy installation, or like some orderly giant was at play with his blocks. These granite chunks protect the perimeter of the Donald C. Cook Nuclear Plant's land.

When Ben and I saw the barriers of the plant on the beach, we went up into the wooded dunes on a neighborhood access path. There, frogs were croaking in competition with the road noise from I-94. Those same massive, white stones appeared and continued out to the highway. I was hoping that we'd have another opportunity to cross back to the lake that day, but the next overpass was our stopping point, so we ended up walking the rest of the day on the Red Arrow Highway. Not the most scenic place to walk, but we did take a nice break on a felled tree where we had a view of the dunes of Grand Mere State Park and the lake beyond.

The next day we woke to the sound of rain, but it stopped by the time we were ready to walk. The rain had scrubbed the air clean and the "negative ion" smell was fantastic that morning. Any time we passed a pine or cedar tree or freshly cut wood the smells were sharp, distinct and fresh.

We headed straight for the nearest public access for the lake, and were disappointed to find that we were on a bluff with a sheer drop to massive rocks. We continued north, taking repeated detours to see if a strip of shoreline had replaced the rocks. These detours turned the 6-mile walk to the town of St. Joseph into a 10-mile wiggly trek, and we didn't have any luck finding lakeshore until we finally hit Silver Beach. Along the way, though, we had some stunning views of the lake, and at one point passed a grove of maple trees being tapped for their spring sap.

After walking the length of Silver Beach, we crossed the drawbridge over the St. Joseph River, one of the main rivers to drain from west Michigan into the lake, and entered the city of Benton Harbor.

A Tale of Two Cities

The slim St. Joseph River separates the cities of St. Joseph and Benton Harbor, but they might as well be on different planets. St. Joseph on the south side of the river is a primarily white community, a lovely tourist town with shops and restaurants and kid-friendly Silver Beach. Benton Harbor on the north side is a primarily black community, with a gutted economic base, and a huge crime and drug problem.

The year before I began the Lake Trek, I was called up for jury duty for federal court in Kalamazoo. We potential jurors watched a video on the importance of our service, something I still appreciate even after being called up for jury duty five or six times (honestly, I've lost count). After the video, we were guided upstairs to a large, federal courtroom. There were over fifty of us there, all white. The judge instructed us on the particulars of the case, involving two defendants from Benton Harbor accused of possessing large quantities of drugs. The two black men sat on one side of the courtroom with their attorneys. On the other side there were five white men and one white woman, all in suits. They were from various federal and state agencies – the FBI, DEA, and State Police – who had spent hundreds of hours and who knows how many tens of thousands of tax dollars catching these two alleged mid-level drug dealers. The witness list for the prosecution was over a hundred people.

The judge spent a long time asking us many questions to probe how everyone felt about the drug laws. On and on, the potential jurors called up to the juror box gave the expected answers.

All this time, I was sitting there thinking about Benton Harbor. About the hopelessness of failed schools, boarded-up stores, and broken families. I wondered how taking two drug dealers off the street – or even a dozen more like them – would change that city. Without fixing the schools and the stores and the families, without giving some hope to that shattered community, there would always be a vacuum that drugs would fill.

You might expect me to say that there was a river dividing that courtroom, but that would be cliché. It was a chasm.

Soaring clay cliffs

I had been on Silver Beach many times, but had never been on the beach on the Benton Harbor side. As Ben and I walked, the bluff became a cliff and the staircases were replaced with mechanized lifts to transport people to and from the beach. I had no idea that there was such an elevation differential here, nor had I seen these lifts anywhere else on the lake. The cliffs were a mixture of sand and gray clay. From the looks of them, with multiple little streams cutting their way down the face of the cliffs, they were prone to erosion.

These little streams carried so much clay that the lake was cloudy with the suspended particles. Since we had traveled extra miles in the morning trying to find access to the shoreline, this day took on epic proportions. I was using not one, but two walking sticks by the end, and would have swapped them for a pair of crutches. We ended up walking 22 miles that day.

I was exhausted, but realized I was getting stronger. I could not have managed such a day at the beginning of the trek, nor probably at this stage without Ben at my side.

41

The next day, the first thing we saw was a dead turtle on the beach. He was huge, his intact shell was probably 15 inches across. His shell was smashed, and only broken pieces of it still clung to his mostly eviscerated body. His head and all four arms were still present, as was his tail. I'm not sure what kind of animal could exert such force on the shell, or if he was pushed from one of the tall cliffs to the rocks below.

It was like a turtle crime scene.

The day was brisk, so we didn't pass any beach walkers for many miles until two dogs ran to us and jumped up on our legs. One was a chubby black lab, the other some sort of beagle mix. They were having a grand time with the whole beach open to them: a constantly full and cool drinking source and all the sticks they could ever want to chew.

After visiting with the dogs and having them as companions as we walked up the beach, we reached the barriers at the Palisades Nuclear Power Plant and hiked inland to the Blue Star Highway. All along the perimeter of this plant, spaced about 15 feet apart, were signs that identified the land as a nuclear facility; the warning text included the line, "Personnel are authorized to use DEADLY FORCE" on trespassers. It struck me as strange that the Cook nuclear plant not far down the lake had come up with a more attractive way to keep their facility safe – the white blocks, without such signage – while this one resorted to threatening to shoot everyone, and repeated that every 15 feet. Abutting the power plant's land on the north side is Van Buren State Park, an inviting, rustic place with woods and tall, wooded dunes.

It was good to see the expanse of the lake as we emerged from between two large dunes. As Ben and I walked shoulder-to-shoulder, I pulled an apple out of my pack and handed it to him. I began to pull out a second one, but he took a bite and handed it back. We shared the apple as we walked. There is an intimacy that arises when two people are out in the elements together, exposed. You look out for each other, listen more closely to what they say. Laughter comes easy, and the exhaustion at the end of the day binds you together.

Remains of winter

Up the beach a bit from the park, we started seeing chunks of ice remaining from the winter. Earlier in March, I had been to this part of the lake and witnessed a solid sheet of shelf ice extending out into the lake as far as I could see.

Now, as we walked further north, we came across more and more ice until there was a slab of chunk ice that had melded together along the shoreline. It stretched for a foot or two along the waterline at first, but then built to 10 to 15 feet of slushy, chunky ice that held the water back from the shore. The wind and waves and the curve of the shoreline must have gathered the ice remnants here, because they disappeared after we encountered a wide stream. Ben and I tossed balls of ice up in the air and watched them disintegrate into a shower of slush.

As we approached South Haven, we encountered larger and larger homes – many still being constructed – along the lake. Some communities cordoned off their beach with rock jetties that we scaled. After climbing over two of these, we discovered that the shoreline gave way to rocky hills studded with large chunks of concrete or placed rock to hold back the force of the lake. I was leaning pretty heavily on my walking stick for these last few inland miles, but Ben wanted to jog ahead. At the beginning of this last day, I had offered to jog, but his knee "was a little stiff." Now, after hiking 14 miles in a day (and 125 miles total in the last 11 days), I was stiffening up and the kid was ready to *run* the rest of the way.

The lake gives fruit

It isn't too far from South Haven that a good friend of mine, Joan, has an organic blueberry farm. The entire western coast of the Lower Peninsula of Michigan, in fact, is a fruit belt. In addition to the blueberries, there are apples (over 20 million bushels annually), cherries (over 150 million pounds annually) and peaches (over 12 million pounds annually). Stanley Johnston developed the famous Red Haven peach in South Haven. He crossed and re-crossed different subtypes of peach trees and over the course of his career grew over 20,000 trees.

Of course, it is precisely because of the lake that the fruit industry thrives here. The lake is so large that it determines the weather and precipitation patterns. The land near the water benefits from steady precipitation, which was especially crucial in the era before irrigation was commonplace. The lake moderates the cold winter temperatures for Western Michigan, and the heavy lake-effect snows cover and insulate the roots of the trees through the winter. In the spring, when these snows melt, the water hydrates the soil. And through the summer, the lake also tempers the potential heat to a more moderate climate.

The glaciers that formed the Great Lakes left Western Michigan a rolling, hilly land with a variety of soil types. This encouraged farmers to try to grow many kinds of fruits. They moved them around until they found precisely where each crop grew best. Cherries thrive in the area around Traverse City, the "Cherry Capital of the World," and also created a great place to cultivate wine grapes. Blueberries do better in the southwest part of the state, while apples do well in the middle.

As of 2006, Michigan still had over 125,000 acres planted with fruit. These acres, however, are in close proximity to the lake. Many farmers are selling to developers because the land is so valuable; they can retire on the money. And if their kids aren't returning to continue the family legacy of hard work on the farm, who can blame them?

Ben and I made it into South Haven along the bluff, passing the first crocuses of spring pushing out of the winter-hardened soil. We met up with Phil and, sinking into the car seats and gratefully loosening laces on boots, allowed tired feet to relax, we began the long drive home as the sun settled into the lake behind us.

Segment 3

April 6–10
South Haven to Grand Haven
With Lucas
50 miles in 4 days

Total Trek Mileage: 175 miles total

Crazy weather, crazy mom

Thankfully, I had over a week off before heading back to the Lake Trek. My feet were feeling pretty good, my blisters almost healed by the night before my other son, Lucas, and I were to hike during his spring break. That night before the next leg, the forecast was for snow. Not a light dusting of snow, but several inches. An old-fashioned Midwestern April snowstorm.

And wind.

Not a light breeze, either. The forecast was for sustained winds over 25 mph.

My brother Phil is a weather nay-sayer. He predicted it would miss us or not materialize at all, that it would disappear from all the fancy weather radar systems. I wanted to believe him, but when it began sleeting around midnight I revamped my plans. I cut the first day's trek from 17 miles down to 5.

By the next morning, six inches of wet snow had fallen. It was so heavy that the lovely redbud tree in front of our house split in two from the weight of snow on its branches. The wind wasn't so bad, but I knew it would be stronger on the lake. And it was cold, a wet cold.

In part, I was thinking of Lucas when I had decided to shorten the first day. I didn't want to discourage him by a horrible start to the experience.

Lucas was excited about the Lake Trek. He'd already started spring training to run track (and had done soccer the previous fall), so he was in decent shape for the adventure. In truth, maybe he wasn't the one I was worried about.

Phil and my mom drove Lucas and me out to Pier Cove, our starting point for the day. I planned to cover the miles that we'd be skipping by adding a fourth day to this segment. We parked in a wooded area elevated from the lake. Lucas and I stepped out of the car and began putting on extra layers of protective gear, to the ominous sound of waves crashing on the beach below us. But while it was breezy, it wasn't really unpleasant. I had the feeling we were both looking forward to the adventure.

After gearing up, we headed down the wooden staircase to the beach. With each step, the wind and roar of the waves clicked up a notch. I began to laugh, thrilled to be back and excited to see the enormous white-capped waves across the expanse of the lake. It was common to see rolling waves near the shoreline of Lake Michigan, but I had never seen breaking waves of this size all across the water.

The snow had fallen further inland. Rain along the shoreline had wet the sand, keeping it from blowing in the wild winds sustained at 35 mph, with gusts well over 40. That was good, as the angle of the wind was such that it would be in our face the entire time we struggled north.

Between the screaming wind, the roar and crash of the waves, and the fact that Lucas and I each wore several layers of hats and hoods and scarves, we couldn't hear each other unless we shouted with our mouths pressed against the side of the other's head. We used hand signals to indicate resting, taking a drink, and, as we struggled forward, what became Luc's favorite sign: he'd point at me, then circle his ear with his finger for the universal – "You're crazy, Mom!"

We stopped several times along the stretch from Pier Cove to Douglas. It was a relief to hunker down behind a pile of rocks, out of the screaming wind for a few moments. We were thirsty from the exertion of walking into a headwind. When Lucas drained our water bottle, I realized that trying to refill it from the lake would be dangerous. We'd already had to scramble up rocks when especially large surges came after us. There were times when there was no beach to walk because the lake was being pushed well up onto the shore. Some areas that were studded with slabs of concrete were intermittently underwater, and we had to time our quick scramble over them with the rhythm of the waves. With water temperatures not even 40 degrees, any misstep could be disastrous.

Where did you come from?

Even though we only went 5 miles, it seemed like 25. It felt like I had one of those resistance bands around my waist holding me back as I took each step. Maybe Lucas was right. Maybe it was a little crazy to be out here, but I was having the time of my life.

The wind was so strong that it was blowing the tops off waves as they crested. It was so strong that once, as I was struggling up a rise of a small dune, it blew me over onto my back. It was so strong that any time it found a dry patch, it created a sandstorm and we had to walk backward to avoid having our faces blasted.

It was fantastic!

For five miles, fantastic. If we would have tried to make 17, well, maybe not so much. I hated to alter the Lake Trek from its linear progression, but as Lucas and I struggled up the four-story wooden staircase to ascend from the beach and head to our B&B for the night, I was glad I had made the decision to add a day to this segment.

We unwound the scarves from our heads and pulled back our hoods as we walked the block to the B&B. The waves were oddly muffled up on this wooded bluff neighborhood overlooking the wild lake. Our ears were still ringing from the constant roar of the three-hour hike, and Lucas's cheeks and nose were rosy from the wind and cold.

The eyes of the couple who owned the Rosemont Inn B&B widened as we blustered into their office with a rush of wind off the lake. "Where did you come from?" they wanted to know, so we explained we'd walked from Pier Cove along the lake.

"Today?!" they asked, unbelieving.

After chatting and checking in, Lucas and I dropped our packs in our rooms. Flopping on my bed for a moment, I still felt the wind and waves in my bones.

The Art Coast of Michigan

After that first day's weather, any small improvement was delightful. We had to head inland for the beginning of Day Two to get around the Kalamazoo

River that snaked its way between the cities of Douglas and Saugatuck. We would also walk through Saugatuck, one of my favorite lakeshore cities. There are many art galleries there. In fact, the cities of Douglas and Saugatuck together make up what's called the Art Coast of Michigan.

The best thing I ever bought in Saugatuck was a bathtub play set with a giant, mutant, "radioactive" (and glow-in-the-dark) squid and several armed frogmen to fight the evil squid. It was a gift for my cousin Milene's son, Jake. To this day I wish I'd gotten one for myself, too.

Lucas and I strolled shoulder-to-shoulder on the nearly deserted road until we reached the Blue Star Highway. This road had the main bridge needed to cross the Kalamazoo River. As we strolled along these first blocks into Saugatuck, some snow flurries swirled around us, but they didn't last long or amount to much. After a short rest in Pumpernickel's Eatery while they made our packed lunch, we were happy to strike out again, out of town and toward the Saugatuck Dunes State Park where we would head back to the lake.

Since the weather had calmed, Lucas and I were able to talk. It was nice to have an unbroken chunk of time with him, too, and to talk about wider subjects like politics and sports. While Ben loved to read novels, Lucas favored current event magazines like *Time* and *The Week* and political blogs online.

Lucas had recently developed a love of words that hadn't been evident before. When he spoke about something he was passionate about, he became quite articulate. We talked about the Lake Trek a bit, and he gave me some advice. "When you say you have a 'love affair' with the lake, it's a little creepy, Mom," he said. "You can say you love it, and 'are exploring your connection with the lake,' but don't say 'love affair.'"

The kid was probably right. Since I'm a writer, I was pleased that Lucas was beginning a love affair with words. Not that he would express it that way.

Species invade the Great Lakes

Mark, a photographer for the Grand Rapids Press, met up with us at the Saugatuck Dunes State Park. He lives a bit north of there in the city of Holland. Mark came ready to hike with us out to the shoreline. He mentioned fishing with his kids off the pier in Holland and how, over the last few years, the fish they were catching went from perch and sunfish to mostly round goby.

Goby is a fish native to the Black Sea, brought here in ballast water two decades ago. It's a small fish, but Mark said that each year they were catching bigger ones than the year before. The goby has a bit of a "Mr. Limpet" look to it, with bulging eyes and a wide mouth. It's a hungry little guy that reproduces quickly.

There are species in the Great Lakes from the Black and Caspian Seas, Eurasia, and Northern Europe, all transported here in ballast water. A ship visiting a far-off freshwater port takes on water there as ballast. It travels across the Atlantic and enters the Great Lakes system. Remember, the Great Lakes taken together is all one system; barriers like the Niagara escarpment and the St. Mary's river into Lake Superior only slow the spread of invasive species, not necessarily preventing it. At a loading dock, a ship in a Great Lakes port discharges its ballast water to get rid of that weight as it prepares to take on new cargo. These foreign waters – along with any traveling aquatic plants and creatures from far-away lands – are dumped into the Great Lakes.

The most conspicuous of these invasive species along my trek so far had been the zebra mussel. This white-and-black-striped mussel had been discharged into Lake St. Claire (between Lake Huron and the Detroit River) in 1985 and rapidly spread throughout all of the Great Lakes. It eats plankton. Day and night, it filters the plankton.

And the other thing it does is make more zebra mussels. Each mature female can release up to a million eggs per year. Currents and waves broadcast the eggs. It's no wonder they spread throughout the lakes so quickly, changing the lake environment in the process. People living along Lake Erie – long known for its murky, green waters – saw the clarity of the lake improve drastically after the mussels made a home there. Clearer waters mean more sunlight getting to the algae and lake plants. Around some Lake Erie marinas, now, because the zebra mussels allow more light to reach the plants which therefore grow faster, they've had to hire people to comb the thick water plants out of the inlets because they choke the waterways. The zebra mussels are also taking food out of the gaping mouths of small fish, competing with them for the tiniest morsels. And the invasive, deeper water quagga mussel is even more voracious than the zebra mussel.

It's difficult to imagine how abundant with life the lakes were even a hundred years ago. Some species, like the blue pike that filled the waters of Lake Erie, are gone forever. Other native species, like the giant lake sturgeon, are endangered.

When Lucas and I walked the lakeshore, the only obvious evidence of this disrupted ecosystem were the zebra mussel shells that weren't there when I was his age. Walking on the sandy shore, however, I couldn't look beneath the waves to see the devastation below. On a sunny day, it seems that all is well with the lake, but that is an illusion. If you know where and how to look and what to measure, the Great Lakes are a battered, blundered, trashed and invaded ecosystem that needs to be strengthened. How? A good start would be a law that all ballast water must be treated before it is discharged to prevent any future invading species from assailing the lakes. Restoring rivers so that native species can better repopulate the lake would be another. Cleaning up toxic spills of the past and preventing future dumping into the lakes is another big one.

This may seem like a tall order, but the lakes should be a place of rich and diverse life under the waves, not of devastation, poisons, and death. On the first segment of my Lake Trek, I have seen the most clear evidence of the toxic side of the lake; as I walked around the southern, industrialized edge, I did not even consider for a moment taking a drink from the waters there. There was a smell coming from the water at times, a sheen of chemicals sometimes visible on the surface.

I recalled one sunny, summer day several years ago. I was walking the beach near Saugatuck and saw a large salmon swimming near the beach. I waded out a few steps, expecting it to swim off into deeper waters with a flick of its thick tail, but instead it swam lethargically toward me. I got close enough to take hold of the fish. This was a strange moment, because fish don't normally allow this.

It felt normal to me; its scales were shiny and it had no obvious injuries. Its flanks were firm and its fins intact. I turned and pushed it into deeper water. It disappeared for a moment, then drifted back toward me. Something was terribly wrong. Had enough PCBs accumulated in its tissues to incapacitate it? Maybe it ate a bunch of smaller fish that had fed on tiny fish that had been eating toxin-laced plankton. Manmade chemicals bioaccumulate; that is, they gather in one creature until that creature is eaten by another, who then takes on that toxic burden.

It all adds up to a terrible truth.

Today, there is a general advisory about eating fish out of the Great Lakes: don't eat them at all if you are a pregnant or nursing woman, or if you are a child. For the rest of the population, don't eat these fish more than once a week. It angers me that we've polluted the lakes to this point.

Big Red and Wrong-Way Rick

The photographer took photos of Luc and me eating lunch in the state park, then walking on the beach a bit. He even took a photo of me holding a handful of zebra mussel shells. We said good-bye to him and continued up the windy beach toward Holland. We could see the lighthouse in the distance, nicknamed "Big Red" (it's boxy and painted red), as we walked up the blustery beach.

We had planned to meet Rick, a reporter for the *Grand Rapids Press*, at a restaurant in Holland. As Luc and I neared the lighthouse, we walked off the beach, then snaked through the neighborhood trying to find our way to the restaurant. This was the first time I got off the beach into an area that was not mapped on my GPS, so we headed in the general direction of the restaurant, but soon found ourselves on a hill at a dead end. I finally got a cell signal there and called Rick. Turned out he was also lost.

The reporter confessed to the nickname "Wrong-way Rick" (due to his lack of directional skills), but vowed to drive toward us as we walked toward him, both of us talking on our cell phones, trying to make sense of where the other one was located.

After a comedy of directional blunders and cell-phone dead spots, Lucas and I located an intersection with named streets, and sat there while Rick got directions from a dog walker to our spot, a few blocks away. It was great to see Rick pull up, and humorous to have to navigate him back to where he had been. He had definitely earned the nickname, and it may have been a miracle that we had found each other at all.

Over hot drinks, Rick interviewed me about why I was doing this Lake Trek. He kept probing and prodding, trying to get at the heart of the matter. Honestly, at this point, I had sketched a growing list of reasons to undertake the adventure, and all were important to me.

1. To have an adventure with a beginning, middle, and end.
2. To explore the connection that I feel with the lake.

3. To explore *all* of the lake, to know it step-by-step; to walk the geology.
4. To do an "American Walkabout," a personal quest where I reconnect with myself and evaluate my life.
5. To explore the environmental challenges that the lake faces and shed some light on those issues.
6. To get to know the communities surrounding the lake and their histories.
7. To challenge myself both physically and mentally.

"But which is most important?" Rick asked.

I looked down at my hands wrapped around my cup of coffee. I felt the warmth radiating through the mug and slowly penetrating my cold hands. I tried to sort through the list, to put it in some kind of order. Perhaps I was a little dizzy from the miles we've walked in the cold to now being inside, so warm, out of the wind.

"They all are." Perhaps I was a little miffed to be pressed for a mission statement after hiking all day. When I was walking, it all made sense. Or it was beyond sense, at some existential sense of being there, next to the Lake, part of something larger than words or lists.

"Well, I think I'll angle my article towards taking on an adventure. That might inspire other people."

"Sure, that's great."

"So," he said, looking up from his notes, "how are you funding this?"

I hadn't expected the question. "Well, since my husband isn't keen about it coming out of our family budget, I'm funding it myself. I've made a little bit of money publishing my short stories, and I have some savings."

I thought back to when Jim had taken his stand about the Lake Trek, how he didn't feel it made sense to walk for days and weeks, with all the costs of lodging and meals and travel, for some result so hard to measure or predict. I took it as a challenge – fine, I had savings, I'd pay for it myself – and continued my planning and training. I knew that he thought I'd simply abandon the adventure, but that – to me – was unthinkable.

After the interview, Phil drove us to the City Flats Hotel in Holland. It was the only hotel in West Michigan to be awarded the Gold LEED (Leadership in Energy and Environmental Design) certificate for being a "green" hotel. I wanted to check it out; the idea of a business built to have a minimal impact on the environment fit in nicely with my adventure.

While Phil, Lucas and I were eating dinner that night, Wrong-Way Rick called my cell phone to ask some follow-up questions.

"I don't want it to seem self-indulgent," he explained, obviously still worried about how to present the rationale for such a journey. "You just taking off and walking around the lake. I don't want people to be upset with you."

"I could have gone to a fancy spa for a few weeks," I countered, "and it might cost as much. But that's not something I'd do."

Self-indulgent? It had been tough so far, and would get tougher. I thought about the long miles already behind me, the headwinds, my toe-nail popping off, the blisters, my swollen feet. I remembered that I was only beginning this quest; that I was still exploring my resolve to complete the Lake Trek, all 1,000 miles, trying to measure if I was strong enough to complete it. And I was only beginning to delve into the complexity of the lake and my connection to it.

It bothered me that I had to justify taking this time for me, to do something that I loved. Was it because it was so close to home, that it wasn't exotic enough? Or was it because I was a woman? If a man had taken time off work to do it, or something else – to going sailing for a month or climb a peak in the Himalayas – would there have been these questions? I was, in fact, taking time from my work of being a wife and mother, and time away from my fiction writing, to do this.

In my mind I argued that I had worked while my husband was in school, then continued to work while he was in his residency. I'd even gone back to work – and school for my Masters degree – after having each of my kids, only being able to stay home with them when my husband finally got a job. Didn't that count for anything?

Phil and Lucas sat across from me at the table while I defended myself to Rick on the phone. When I hung up, exasperated – not at Rick, but at society's dim view of the worth of mothers and walking – I noticed that my brother Phil was smirking.

"What?" I asked.

"You know what the headline is going to be." He fought to hold back laughter.

"What?"

"RICH BITCH WALKS BEACH." Phil burst into laughter, and Luc and I cracked up. We laughed so long and so hard that I had time to take photos of both Phil and Luc turning red and trying to catch their breath.

Hilarious.

Crossings

The next day, Phil drove us around Lake Macatawa to the north side of its outlet into Lake Michigan. The sand looked extra white because it was covered with a scrim of frost. I hadn't seen this so far on the trek, so it must have been the perfect temperature and humidity. I'd certainly had colder days.

As the sun climbed in the sky it erased the frost it touched, while areas still in shadow remained crisp white. Where there were irregular shadows, intricate frost paintings took shape on the sand.

Lucas and I clipped along at a good pace, with only one backpack between us since we were able to consolidate supplies for this last day. Periodically along the wide beach, streams would wind their way to the lake. The first one we reached this day was wide and knee-deep, so I pulled out the garbage-bag waders. When I reached the other side, I stepped out of the bags, tied them to my walking stick, and tossed it back to Lucas.

"What do you want me to do with these?" he asked.

"Put them on and wade."

"I can jump this."

I looked at the width of the stream again and at the soft edge where I had emerged. "Just wade it."

"Why? I can jump it."

"The sides are too soft to land safely." I gave him the "mom stare." He exhaled a groan, thrashed the bags onto his legs, and crossed. He pulled the bags off and handed them back to me with the stick.

"Happy?" he asked.

"Hey, if it was a warm day, I'd have let you jump it. Getting doused wouldn't matter. That water is freezing."

Lucas huffed off ahead of me and I let him put a little distance between us. As a toddler, Luc thought running toward the road was fun because that was one way to be sure I'd chase after him. He was a risk-taker, head-strong, and could argue the injustice of any punishment with barrister-like passion.

When Lucas reached the next stream, he leapt it without glancing back, then stood defiantly on the far side watching me approach. I can only say that I was relieved to find the width of the stream was – I was pretty sure – within my leaping capabilities. I ran up to it, launched into the air, and landed next to him with my arms held high and a big "Ta-da!" look on my face. His scowl cracked, then we laughed together, the tension broken.

Lucas took hold of the backpack.

"What do you need?" I asked, thinking he was trying to get something from inside.

"Let me carry it," he said.

It was liberating to be free of it, and nice to have my strong son at my side.

I've walked 150 miles

Luc and I headed inland at the channel at Port Sheldon. There is a massive coal-burning power plant there. As we wound inland on dirt roads, I kept an eye on my GPS unit, because I knew I was approaching 150 miles of the trek. At the very step I reached that mark, I had Lucas take my photo.

I was happy. "I've walked 150 miles."

"Yaaay. Only 850 to go!" was Luc's reality-check reply.

We made our way inland and north for several miles to get around the power plant, then cut back to the lake at Kirk Park. This is a place I had visited often during my college years and being there brought back nice memories. Jim and I had picnicked there when we were dating, and I mentioned this to Lucas. He seemed stunned at the idea of his parents dating at some point in the past. He probably thought, like most kids, that time began when he was born. Or, maybe, he had a hard time envisioning us at about his age, falling in love.

I thought about that young couple, now over two decades in the past. I thought about all the decisions and challenges that had been spread out before me – Marriage? Kids? Grad school? Where would I live? What profession would I finally choose? I don't think my younger self needed an adventure like the Lake Trek because life, back then, was a daily adventure.

We walked to the parking lot where Phil was waiting. I had asked him to stop by in case Lucas was too tired to go any further. Luc was doing pretty well, but he opted for lunch with Phil, while I finished the remaining miles alone to Grand Haven.

It was one of those crystalline clear days where you can see things in more detail, like an extra dimension has opened to you. Where the wind feels alive as it swirls and swoops around you and the lake speaks through the waves reaching toward your feet. There is clarity in the air and this translates into clarity of thought and emotion.

This was the perfect time in my life, I thought, to be here doing this. It was *necessary.* I felt my younger self cheering for me. During the remaining hours on the beach, I had the chance to talk to that younger self, then to bridge the decades between us and find that she still resided within me. She was happy with what our life had become, and I discovered that I was content with the decisions she had made along the way.

Phil is the Lake Trek Transporter

We drove home, and I returned Lucas to the rest of his spring break. He had developed two blisters that last day and wanted to let them heal before he got back to running track. I took off to return to the lake the very next day, though, to finish the miles that Lucas and I had skipped over that first stormy day.

As I walked, I noted that there were several stretches of a narrow, rocky beach with a vertical hill next to it – spots that would have been deeply submerged in the storm on that earlier day. So, I was pleased that I had made the decision to leave this section for a day with friendlier weather.

I had designated Phil my "Lake Trek Transporter." When I told him this, he mentioned that he would shave his head and start kicking people like in those "Transporter" action movies. He was waiting for me at the park where Lucas and I had begun three days earlier. Returning to that bend of beach with hardly a ripple on the lake was surreal compared to the roaring, living thing it had been just three days earlier. I took a photo and later set it side-by-side with one shot during the storm. I could see that the lake had been pushed up the beach at least 20 feet from its calm level. It was a true *seiche,* a monumental, standing wave.

Segment 4

May 6–10
One Day with Mary
Two Days with Les & Milene
Grand Haven to Ludington
75 miles in 5 days

Total Trek Mileage: 250 miles

Studying the work of the wind

A little more than an hour's hike north of Grand Haven, I entered the P. J. Hoffmaster State Park. This park preserves several miles of shoreline and over 1200 acres of dunes and forest. This park came about through the efforts of P. J. Hoffmaster and E. Genevieve Gillette, who were friends. He was the superintendent of state parks in Michigan in the 1920s and 1930s, and then headed up the DNR for the next two decades. Gillette was the first woman to graduate from Michigan State University's landscape architecture class. Hoffmaster charged Gillette with scouting out areas that would make good parks. What a dream job!

While the park north of Grand Haven is the only one to bear their names, they teamed up to create and secure funding for many of Michigan's finest parks.

Visiting the shores of Lake Michigan through the years, I was used to seeing the undulating dunes, the wide sandy beaches, the wooded inland dunes that no longer wandered with the wind. In the Gillette Nature Center, there are a series of displays showing how the dunes were formed. It also explains why they are here in West Michigan. How after the glaciers had ground rocks to sand, winds and waves worked together for thousands of years to loft and shape the dunes. How plants helped to catch and keep grains of sand in place, enabling the dunes to rise.

A section of the beach and dunes in the park was roped off as a research area. The scientist in charge happened to teach at Calvin College where Ben was attending – so I arranged to have lunch with her.

I read up on Dr. Deanna van Dijk's work before meeting with her. She is an aeolian/coastal geomorphologist. Aeolus was the Greek god of wind; aeolian means having to do with wind. Dr. van Dijk's studies how the wind "played" and shaped and formed and destroyed Michigan's coastal dunes. For over a decade, she's been studying how to protect and preserve these sand formations. In her papers, she is able to express dune growth and migration in mathematic language.

Okay, I admit it, I'm a bit of a science nerd, and I was appropriately geeked about meeting her.

Over lunch, I have trouble deciding what to ask first. "You have the best job," I finally say. "You are required to spend time out on the lakeshore."

"Well, in the late fall at least," she says. "That's when we set the instruments. Then we take measurements until early spring, before people are out there disrupting the dunes. I'm in the office most of the rest of the year, trying to make sense of the data. And teaching, of course."

"The dunes probably change the most in the winter with all that wind."

"They do. It wasn't too long ago that scientists thought the dunes were stable during the colder months."

I think back to the first day on the lake with Lucas, how we had been sandblasted with the strong winds. "Seriously? Hadn't they ever been on the shore during a winter storm?"

"I know," she laughs.

"How did you end up playing in the sand?"

"I did my grad work in Ontario, and my advisor's work was on the dunes of Lake Ontario. When I came to teach at Calvin, I looked for similar research done on the Lake Michigan dunes and discovered that there wasn't much. When I asked questions about how the dunes moved and changed here, people didn't know the answers."

"So, the field was wide open."

"Yes. I was looking for a niche, and so little basic research had been undertaken." She goes on to explain the instruments she uses to track the dunes. Some are as simple as a wooden dowel sunk into the dune, marking the level of the sand in the fall. In the spring, she could measure how many inches had been added or taken away. Other devices were more elaborate, such as a trap to gather sand blown over a surface.

She also tells me about a large dune near the town of Holland, between a campground and the lake. She made recommendations that informed the plan to restore and protect the dune while still allowing foot traffic from the campground to the beach.

"It's gratifying to know that my research is being applied to real-life preservation projects like that," she says.

As I hiked toward Muskegon, I studied my maps. Muskegon has parks north and south of the Muskegon River, which connects Lake Michigan and Muskegon Lake, an inland lake that divides the city. It is a city of water, and, to its credit, they've set aside huge tracts of shoreline as parks.

Unfortunately, industry consumed Muskegon's largest dune, Pigeon Hill, some decades ago. It was carted off between the mid-1930s to mid-1960s, mostly to make castings for molten metal. The base of this dune used to occupy 40 acres. It was called Pigeon Hill because thousands of passenger pigeons would rest there during their migration. Some enterprising businessman purchased the dune, set up a conveyor to ships waiting on the lake, and had steam shovels slowly eat away at the mountain of sand. There are condos on the site, which is now an incredibly flat piece of land. I felt like there should have been a dotted line in the sky where this massive dune once stood.

The shoreline became impassable north of the water intake station for the city of Muskegon, so I headed inland. Thankfully, someone was working inside the pumping station, and they had left the gate open in the eight foot, barbed wire-topped fence. After I had hiked about a mile, I was able to stroll through the open gate, taking a shortcut onto surface streets that led me five miles into town. Had the gate not been open, I would have had to backtrack at least a mile.

Muskegon was a lumber town. In the mid-1800s it was known as the "Lumber Queen of the World." At its peak, over 500 million feet of lumber were cut annually. When I think of this period in the Great Lake's history, the vision I see in my mind is one of stump-filled fields.

Of course, the thick forests must have seemed endless to the early settlers.

It's difficult to envision it now, but in those lumbering days the best way to travel around Michigan was by water, not land. The master river men would ride the logs for miles on the inland rivers leading to the port towns. Their job, and a difficult one it proved, was to herd the logs after the winter logging to the mills in the early spring, when the waters ran high – preventing jams, prying stray logs away from snags. Often, the river men would not set foot on land for many days, except to eat and sleep. The most accomplished of them could even ride the rapids on the logs, a balletic feat akin to driving a herd of cattle while standing atop their backs.

A gourmet lunch on the beach

The next day my friend Mary drove me to the state park on the north side of the river. She married one of my husband's best friends just after college, and she and I hit it off right away. Their oldest daughter is the same age as Lucas, so both our photo albums are filled with shots of the kids growing up together. Mary has shoulder-length blond hair, laughing blue eyes, and she wouldn't be able to swear if you paid her.

At the park, I watched her heave her backpack out of her trunk.

"That's a big pack for a day hike," I said.

It was bigger than mine, and I was hiking for five days.

"Oh, I made a special lunch," she answered. "I made homemade crackers with flax seed, tomatoes and spices. And I have herbed cream cheese, and apples—"

"And the wine?" I joked.

"Oh my word! Of course! A tiny bottle!"

We cracked up. We have tried to "out-gourmet" each other over the years, always cooking something new or buying special foods when we'd get together.

The day was cool, and the foghorn sounded as we walked along the channel to the lake. The dense fog took the edges off everything: trees, dunes, waves, even sounds. It was like being enfolded in soft, cotton batting. The fog rolled inland in billowing pulses. Dunes and trees emerged from the mist as we walked. Little green beetles had recently hatched by the thousands, and hundreds of them were lying dead on the beach.

It was nice to have uninterrupted time to talk with Mary, but there were also many small, black flies out that day. The person talking invariably swallowed an especially adventurous fly. The subsequent coughing disrupted the conversational flow, but it was so comical that we started keeping track of how many each of us had ingested.

We stopped to share Mary's lunch. Taking our packs off, we made ourselves comfortable on a driftwood log. Mary pulled out containers of food and set up a little buffet between us. I laughed when she ceremoniously pulled out the little bottle of white wine and two tiny cups.

We had gone probably five miles by this time. As I spread a homemade cracker with cream cheese, I asked Mary, "You doing okay?"

"I'm a little sore, but not bad."

"Let me know whenever you want to take a pause. I want the day to be fun for you, not like a forced march."

"Thanks."

I lifted my tiny cup of wine. "This is delightful."

We tapped our plastic cups together.

She got quiet for a moment, and I thought that she was listening to the gentle waves, but then she said, "I've been having weird symptoms for awhile now. My doctor has ruled out just about everything except autoimmune diseases. He's going to test for those next."

I asked how she is doing with it, how her family is coping.

"It's not too bad. I tire easily, sometimes I'm really sore."

She still seemed upbeat, glad to be hiking the lakeshore with me. I thought of my challenges of the Lake Trek: the planning, the obstacles, the problem-solving that came with each day's hike. Blisters, leg cramps, scrapes and scratches are minor problems compared to Mary's strange symptoms and the worry that accompanied them.

Mary is one of the nicest people I know

When we got near Duck Lake, we climbed the dune up to a road. We followed it over the wide stream that snaked its way from Duck Lake to join up again with the waters of Lake Michigan. Along the way, there was a crazy dog chasing cars. It was having a great time, but it nearly got hit twice while we were watching. It was so friendly that managed to loop Mary's sweatshirt underneath its collar as a leash. We found a name on the dog's tag – Georgia – and a phone number. Mary pulled out her cell and dialed.

"Hello, my friend and I found your dog at Duck Lake Park."

Mary listens for a moment. "Oh my word! Is this Ruthie? This is Mary!"

Of course, Mary knows the owner.

"Yes! We'll take her home for you. No problem."

No problem? I think. The dog must live the way we're heading. That's the only way it's "no problem." There was something about backtracking made my muscles ache, my legs feel leaden. Walking with the lake on my left, everything was great, every joint felt oiled, every muscle toned and strong. Well, almost that good.

Mary gets directions to the house, then hangs up and grins at me. "That was Ruthie!"

"So I gathered," I laugh.

"They live real close." Mary points back the way we've come. "A quarter mile or so, and then up a big hill."

These sentences have many bad words in them: *a quarter mile* the wrong way, *up a big hill.* Better words: *right over there, the way we're heading* and *down that hill, right by the lake,* and *she told me where she keeps the gourmet chocolate.*

Have I mentioned that Mary is one of the nicest people I know?

We walk Georgia back to her house. The dog's blue-purple tongue lolls out of her mouth; I wonder what she could have eaten to give it that color. Georgia is happy to walk with us, but her eyes follow every passing car like she is missing a great chase. We walk into Ruthie's neighborhood, and Mary leads to the base of the largest hill in sight.

She points. "They live at the top."

"Of course they do," I mutter. The hill is so steep that we have to walk on our toes all the way up the paved driveway. It's *cartoon* steep.

Inside the house we refill our water bottles as I look around the kitchen. The kids have left some sort of blue-purple cereal out: tongue color solved. Georgia stretches out in the living room for her afternoon nap in a patch of sunshine, and we leave.

At the bottom of the hill, Mary notices that she has forgotten her sweatshirt. I tell Mary to have a seat and rest, and I retrieve it. Yep, I get to walk that cartoonishly steep hill twice.

We retrace our steps to the other side of the stream and head back down to the lake on wide, wooden stairs. As we descend from the road, the fog closes in on us, and the temperature drops ten degrees. Since the wind has shifted and is now in our faces, the fog quickly condenses on my glasses. Between the condensation and the thick fog, I can't see more than a few yards.

With the temperature drop, the fog also condenses on our clothing and hair. It is like being wrapped in a damp towel. We begin walking the distance between Duck Lake and White Lake. Soon, the beach disappears and is replaced with a series of seawalls abutting the hillside. I know that there is more beach up ahead near the White River lighthouse, but I don't know how much further it is, and I can't see very far in the fog.

I tell Mary to have a seat and I scout ahead. The water deepens near the seawalls and I have to walk on the top of them, balancing, creeping along. I am getting tired, so I know that Mary is probably exhausted, and climbing seawalls is much more taxing than strolling on a packed sand beach. The walking has been tough for much of the day because where the sand was well packed, it was steeply angled toward the water. I can feel blisters forming on the sides of my heels.

After struggling along for a hundred yards or so, I turn back. I don't want to subject Mary to all that climbing and balancing, and I still haven't found the beach. The fog has gotten even thicker during the last half hour, so we must follow our tracks in the sand to find our way back to the stairs.

Once we go just 100 yards inland and then up the 20 vertical feet of steps to the road, we leave the thick fog behind us down on the lake. Up on the road it is a completely different weather day; the sun has come out and the sky is bright blue. We can look down and see the hovering fog, but it sticks to Lake Michigan, velcroed there by the mass of cold water. Out in the sunshine, we feel like we have time-traveled to a different day.

We begin walking the last mile to White Lake and Mary calls her husband to pick us up. After retrieving Mary's car back in Muskegon, who should we pass on the road by Duck Lake but that crazy dog, Georgia, running free again, chasing cars!

Dave and Mary live in Montague, the sister city of Whitehall. The two cities reside on opposite sides of White Lake. These are both pleasant lake towns, but there is a legacy of toxic industry in the area that, even today, leaves a mark on the land, the people, and the lake.

Whitehall's Eagle Tanning Works was established on the banks of White Lake just after the Civil War. Nearby hemlock forests provided bark used to process the hides in the early years. The tannery operated for over 100 years on the shores of the inland lake, first supplying leather for horse-drawn buggy seats, and then quality leather to the car industry.

The cleanup of the 33-acre site has been ongoing for over a decade. Thousands of old hides had to be dredged from the bottom of White Lake. When a hide did not meet standards, it was dumped into the lake along with all leather trimmings. In addition, there are "waste lagoons" on the property that still contain decades of toxic tanning chemicals.

I could list the chemicals here; they all have scary names like ferrous sulfate (also called pickle acid) and sodium hydrosulfide. I think it's better to demonstrate what happens when these two chemicals are inadvertently mixed. There was an accident at the Whitehall tannery in 1999 where a tanker full of sodium hydrosulfide solution was mistakenly hooked up to where the pickle acid was stored. These two solutions reacted, forming hydrogen sulfide, a poisonous gas. The fallout from this mistake was one fatality, one injury, an evacuation of the plant, and almost a half-million dollars in damage.

The sludge in the waste lagoons is so toxic that there is a valid argument to leaving it in place so as not to release contaminates into the air when moving it. Developers are working to clean up the site so they can convert it into a condo community called Tannery Bay.

In addition to having this industry on the shores of White Lake, the area hit the mother lode in bad decisions for the environment when they courted Hooker Chemical to build a plant there. If Hooker doesn't ring a bell, maybe Love Canal will. Same company. In their Montague plant they produced compounds used in the pesticide class that includes DDT.

I could go on for a long time about this site – how much was dumped, how jobs were put before the environment, and much more – but it makes me heartsick. Let me just tell you about the clean-up that Hooker had to do in the past and continues to this very moment. A vault was created to entomb over a million cubic yards of chemical waste. The bottom and sides are lined with 10-foot-thick, packed clay walls, and all of the barrels of toxic waste and contaminated soil was trucked inside the vault. Then, the trucks used to haul the waste were parked inside because they were so heavily contaminated. The vault was then sealed with concrete.

The cleanup continues today. Hooker has an on-site facility to pump up the groundwater, filter it, then pipe it back underground. They've been doing this continuously after an out-of-court settlement in 1979. That's over three decades of trying to clean the contaminated ground water. The pump buildings and the vault are the only two Hooker structures left on the almost 900-acre, fenced site. Oh, and there are security personnel there.

After spending the night with Mary's family in Montague, Mary and I hop into her car so she can drive me to the north side of White River to continue my trek.

"Do you want to see the Hooker vault?" she asks.

"If it's not too far out of your way."

"Nope, it's right over there." She makes a right turn. A tall fence runs alongside the narrow road.

I gasp. Not at the vault, because it is difficult to see in the distance through the trees, but because we've only traveled a couple of miles from her house. She slows the car, but keeps it rolling.

"On that hillside, can you see something whitish? It's hard to see from here, and impossible once the trees leaf out." She points and I follow her line of sight.

"I think so."

"It's five stories tall, but it's a long way off." She does a slow U-turn to go back to the road that will take us out to the lake. "If we stop here, the security guys will come out."

"Even if we're on the road?"

"Yes. One time Dave was doing a marathon, and the route took them along here. I drove out with bottles of water to hand to the runners as they passed. I parked over there, across the road from Hooker land. I wasn't there three minutes before they sent out a guy in a truck to tell me to move on."

"How can they do that? They don't own the road."

"They do it all the time. I explained about the race, but they didn't care."

I am amazed that my friends had built a house so near this site. "Did you know about this when you bought the land?"

She shakes her head.

"The sellers didn't tell you?"

"Not a word," she says.

We hug goodbye on the walkway along White River and I try to enjoy the glorious, sunny day. I try to not think about the chemical history of this area. Mary snaps a few photos of me and I wave as I walk out to the broad, pristine-to-the-eye beach.

This is the first day warm enough to wear shorts, so I zip off my pant legs – and shield my eyes from the glare of my winter-white legs. This is also the first day that the ladybugs are out en masse on the lakeshore, swarming over pieces of driftwood and the occasional fish skeleton. The adventurous black flies, thankfully, had disappeared with the fog.

Danger at Flower Creek

I had a smooth hike on a wide beach and even jogged part of it over the first two hours up to Flower Creek. With a name like that, it seemed logical to merely wade to the other side, but it actually turned out to be a rather deep channel, over twenty feet wide near the lake. It took a jog parallel to the shoreline, though, and a narrow sandbar spit had formed between the creek and the lake.

I walked out on the sandbar, studying the moving water. The creek flow sped up near the end of the spit, where it narrowed before joining the lake. The lake waves churned on the other side.

As I neared the point, I determined that the creek was not shallow enough to wade, and I saw that it was too wide to jump. I took one more step toward the point and the sand suddenly got mushy, then began to slough off beneath my feet, dropping in wide slabs. I stumbled, soaking one boot, and almost falling into the deep, rushing waters.

I leapt away from the brink, back-pedaling for all I was worth, and barely made it back to safety.

I was so intent on figuring out how to cross the rushing water of Flower Creek that I had lost track of the peril of walking out on the sandy point. This was a moment when the Lake Trek could have taken a horrible turn.

As the creek rushed out to the lake through the narrowed outlet, it slimmed there at the point, which meant the volume of water was deeper and moving faster. It was probably ten feet deep. If a bit more of the point had sloughed off underneath me, I would have been instantly dumped into the fast, cold water, headed out into the lake.

My sling pack would have ensured my ride on the bottom of the creek, at least until I could have taken it off. I would have had to release the clasp in front to be free of the fifteen pounds. I would have lost my pack as it would have continued out into the lake even as I swam back to shore. My glasses would have continued on without me, too, along with my back-up pair tucked safely in my lake-bound pack.

This time, I was lucky.

I thought about all this as I stood on the wide base of the spit of sand that ended at that dangerous, eroding point. A shiver of fear passed through me, and I resolved to learn from the moment so I didn't make such a blunder in the future. I hadn't even gone one fifth of the way around the lake. There were sure to be many dangerous situations that I'd have to get myself through in the miles that stretched before me.

I headed inland, hoping to find a culvert or road over the creek. Not too far from the lake, the creek opened into a lovely wetland. Lovely in the sense that wetlands are great for the lake. The downside of wetlands is that you have to go around them.

This detour added several miles, but it was a gorgeous day, and I passed many bucolic farms and orchards, their trees alive with blossoms. I also came across patches of trillium in the woods. There's something about seeing a patch of bright, white trillium, something reassuring about spring and life. The blue sky was streaked with high, wispy cirrus clouds, and a slight breeze kept me comfortable in my shorts.

At a campground, I asked if I could pass back to the lake and also inquired about the shore further north up to Silver Lake where I was going to stop for the night. They told me that there is only one river to get around; the rest of the way should be nice beach.

South of where we were, however, they said, the lake between there and Flower Creek was so high that the shore was impassable, with high bluffs dropping straight down to deep water. So, even if I had been able to cross Flower Creek, I would have been forced inland soon after that, or maybe even forced to backtrack – even to re-cross the treacherous outflow.

Dumping in the lake

At the outlet for Stony Lake, I walked inland through a summer camp. The place was completely deserted, but I could imagine the lingering sounds of kids having fun in the cabins, on the trails, in the arts & craft tent, and mess hall. I tried to not think about all the horror movies set in deserted summer camps as I passed through. I crossed over the river and dropped back to the lake.

As I walked along the north side of the river, I was hit with a strong smell of some kind of solvent. It was coming from inland. It seemed like something had been dumped into the river and was flowing out to the lake. I pulled out my phone to call the DNR, but I didn't have a signal, not even a weak one. It was Friday, getting late in the day. I thought about how easy it would be to dump toxic waste at almost any point along the lake or the streams leading out to it. Who would be there to witness it? And if it was reported, would there be any evidence left by the time someone got out to the lake to investigate?

The lake is vulnerable. Industries are regulated today, but they can still get permits to dump toxic sludge into the lake. What would stop someone from dumping a barrel of solvent into a remote stream or river? I had always assumed that there was a social contract, a central morality preventing people from damaging the lake, but how naïve is that?

Personally, if a small candy wrapper blew out of my pocket while hiking, I would run after it until I had secured it once again. The thought of being responsible for littering even on this tiny scale felt like a crime to me.

But industries dump toxic sludge and thousands of pounds of chemicals each day into the lake with permission. Industries and cities treated the lake like a vast sewer before the Clean Water Act. Most people have heard of Cleveland's Cuyahoga River catching fire because of industrial waste, but the Chicago River was doing the same thing decades earlier.

As I stood where the little river joined the lake, the smell dissipated and was gone. I wondered when we will realize how fragile the lake is and how valuable a healthy lake is to everyone.

I arrived at the Little Sable Lighthouse as the sun was lowering in the sky, its reflection a wide, sparkling band on the water. Lighthouses are the friendliest of structures on the lakeshore. This one stands alone, a tall, brown brick tower with a black cap and balcony around the top. The keeper's house was removed long ago. On this day, I was the only person to share the beach with the structure standing tall in the sand.

I took some photos, then headed inland. When I checked my GPS at the end of the day, I was surprised to find that I'd hiked 24.7 miles. The Flower Creek detour had stretched the distance, making it the longest day of the trek so far.

My sister Leslie and cousin Milene met up with me to hike the final two days of the segment. I wanted them to see my favorite lighthouse, so we headed back to Little Sable and watched the sun set. They were giddy after driving for hours, so I took photos while they jumped around barefoot in the sand, chattering over the calls of the gulls. After almost 25 miles of walking, I wasn't quite up to hopping around, so I just smiled and listened.

Shoppers, not hikers

As much as I am a hiker, Les and Milene are shoppers. They had shopped long and hard for their two-day hike. They had even stopped at an outlet mall on their drive north. They are so serious about shopping that they wanted their boots to match their backpacks. Milene (who is just under 5'4") ended up buying a pack that was almost bigger than she is, the kind of pack you'd see a through-hiker carry on the Appalachian Trail. She loved it because the color matched the laces on her boots.

Her boots, however, were still sitting by her front door at home since she had forgotten them in the frenzy to pack all her new, cool gear. The only shoes she had with her were very cute black sandals with white bows. After breakfast the next day, we went shoe shopping. She had to settle for some leather tennis shoes because all the boots they had were steel-toed in large, men's sizes. But Milene was happy to have found something.

We begin hiking from our hotel in the city of Mears back to the lakeshore on the north side of Silver Lake. The rain and the wind pick up as we pass orchards and spiky asparagus fields. The weather report is for winds at 20 mph, but gusts much stronger on the beach. Low whitecaps froth the lake as far as we can see. Surging waves consume the wide beach.

Les and Milene put on brave smiles, and follow me up the shoreline.

Actually, Milene tends to lead, walking quite fast on her little legs.

"Can we get her to slow down?" I jokingly ask Les.

"Nope. She's in 'soldier mode.'"

We stay on the flat part of the beach as much as possible, but the waves often drive us up into the low, rolling dunes. Milene takes a large wave to the feet and has to stop to change her socks. When she pulls off her soggy socks, I notice that her toenail polish matches her backpack.

The small streams have swollen with the rainstorm in the night. Each one is a logistical problem to be solved: Is it narrow enough to jump? Are the banks solid enough to jump off and land on? Is there a downed tree to walk across? Are there planks or limbs we can put into the stream? Or is it shallow enough to wade across with trash-bag waders?

As I watch them jump a small stream, I think: "These are not *stream-jumping* women. These are *shopping* women."

The streams swell as the rain continues to fall. We use the trash-bag waders on one last stream before I decide that we need to head inland to be safe. It was one thing to be out there alone with only me to worry about, but I had two of my favorite people along with me. The day is too cold to risk one of us falling into a stream, and even though Les and Milene are still smiling, I know they are tired.

Heading inland isn't easy, though, as steep dunes flank the shore. I find one with a trail and begin climbing. About halfway up, I look down at Les and Milene at the base of it, staring up at me with "she wants us to walk up there?" looks on their faces.

After a moment of disbelief, they follow.

Pentwater is our stopping point for the day. I had calculated a walk of 11 miles from Mears. This calculation, though, was based on a nonexistent crossing point over the channel of Pentwater Lake.

The bridge we'd need to take instead over the inland lake is over two miles inland from Lake Michigan, then we'd have to hike back along the north side of Pentwater Lake to where we were staying for the night. Les and Milene look wind- and wave-whipped by this time, and I didn't want to break the news of an extra 5 miles for the day, so I just keep walking, trying to navigate the shortest distance possible. We finally reach Pentwater Lake and head east, away from our hotel, to the bridge. My GPS is adding distance to our walk, not taking it away.

Every 20 minutes or so one of my foot-weary companions asks, "How much further?" I keep checking the GPS, but for the next hour, the remaining distance stays the same. Leslie snaps.

"I want to take your GPS," she snarls, "and throw it. Then walk over to it and stomp on it."

I know her feet are sore, so the thought that she will go out of her way to step on the GPS means she is at the end of her rope.

We are supposed to meet a reporter, Andy, at our hotel at four o'clock, but we will not make it by then. I call him and move it to five. As we are approaching the bridge to take us over Pentwater Lake, a truck pulls over and the man rolls down his window and leans out.

"I was wondering how you get around inland obstacles," he says. "So, you just walk? I'm Andy."

"The reporter Andy?" Milene smiles as if witnessing a miracle.

"Oh my god, don't drive away, don't leave," Les mutters under her breath. "Don't leave. Don't leave."

"We take rides from reporters!" I reply.

Les continues to mutter as Andy jumps out and begins clearing things off the back seat.

"I'll ride on the bumper!" Les says as we approached his truck.

We all jump in, saved from those last two torturous miles.

After a photo session back on the beach where the waves are even higher and wind stronger and colder than before, Andy drops us at the Channel Lane Inn, and we collapse for a few moments. Milene finally says, "Happiness . . . is *not* walking!"

We clean up to look presentable for dinner. Les has two requirements for the restaurant. "It has to be close, and I need a stiff drink," she says.

Milene changes into her pretty black sandals with the white bows for the walk to the restaurant. Les and I are a little envious as we put our boots back on. I had told them about my trick to keep my toes happy during the Lake Trek: I put Vaseline between them so they don't build up any friction. Milene had taken this a step further and had put Vaseline all over her feet before putting on her special pairs of hiking socks that she had shopped three stores to find.

"Look," she says as she slips into her pretty sandals, "No blisters! I'm going to win the bet!" Both her husband and her boss had wagered that she'd get blisters.

The day had been tough on us, physically with the cold and wind and rain, and mentally with the added miles due to my miscalculation. The "are we there yet?" feeling of the last five miles was pretty intense, and I knew I barely escaped a bloody mutiny.

At dinner, I pick up a little tub of butter and start to open it to spread it on some bread. "Oh, this should be interesting," Milene says.

"What?"

"Watching what you do with that cream."

I look closer at the little tub. It was made by a butter company, but it was definitely cream for the coffee. "I'm a little tired," I admit.

"Tired!" Les chimes in. "I can't believe how hard this is! If today had been the first 12 miles of 1,000 for me, I would have stopped! What did you hike yesterday? Twenty?"

"Twenty-four point seven," I laugh.

"Yeah," Milene agrees. "We couldn't even talk to each other out there today with all that wind." Milene loves to chat.

"I keep wondering what Grandma would have thought about this," Les says. "No one in her generation would have thought of doing something like this. Even our moms are a little amazed."

"You mean worried," Milene says. "My mom is worried, though she will worry less now that we're with you," she nods at me. "Though I think she went to church twice today to light candles."

"I figure our moms worry so much that I don't have to worry at all," I laugh.

On the way back to the hotel, we notice that the Cosmic Candy Company is still open. Milene orders a bag of caramel corn that is bigger than my head for the next day's hike, while Les and I pick out our favorite candy.

Since I had made the blunder with the Pentwater Lake crossing, I ask the owners, John and Greg, about the lakeshore north of Pentwater. "Is the beach easy to walk from here to Ludington?" I ask.

They look at each other, then back at me.

"Well, there's the power plant."

"Oh, yeah, I saw that on Google Earth. I thought we'd approach it, then cut inland around it."

"You'll need to cut inland before you get close to it," John says. "It's all restricted."

"And the elevation," Greg adds.

"Cut in at Bass Lake outlet," John says.

I nod. I had seen Bass Lake on my maps north of Pentwater and the slender creek that joined it to Lake Michigan.

Leslie's eyes go wide with excitement. "Bass Lake Outlet? Where?"

"Not that kind of outlet, Les," I laugh. "No shopping."

Milene joins us struggling under the weight of her huge bag of caramel corn. "Shopping? Where?" she asks.

Ten-mile people

The next morning, the weather and lake has calmed. Les and Milene seem to have mostly recovered from the battering the day before. We shoulder our packs and walk out to Mears State Park on the north side of the Pentwater channel.

"This is how I thought it would all be," Milene says, looking at the blue sky. "Like when we go to the beach house. A nice stroll on the beach."

"Yeah, not like yesterday's hell," Les adds.

Blue sky, sun, and light winds make the day more enjoyable. There are storm clouds and rain south of us, but they stay there, washing away our footsteps from the day before.

We go inland at Bass Lake to cross over the "outlet," then stay on Lakeshore Road the rest of the way to the pick-up point, north of the massive pumped storage hydroelectric plant. I can see a lot of detail in advance from satellite images, but this day's hike proves to me that I need to start paying more attention to changing elevations in the future, and to the scale of details. The fence surrounding the power plant near the water looked small on the images, but that's because I had no idea about the scale of the turbines near the shore. They are enormous, and that made the fence, topped with barbed wire, much taller than I thought. We stroll underneath high-voltage wires. These wires are strung between two rows of tall, metal towers spaced regularly from the lake, then up the hills inland, marching off into the distance over many miles.

The pumped storage hydroelectric plant is fascinating. It is comprised of an elevated water reservoir on the highest point on the hill. The surface area of the reservoir is about 3 square miles, and it is over 100 feet deep. This holding area is at least another 100 feet higher in elevation from the road we walked, and the road is well above lake level. Massive turbines line the shore. During the night, when electricity prices are lowest and there is extra power on the grid, turbines pump water from the lake uphill into this reservoir. At times of peak usage, the water flows back downhill, through the turbines, generating electricity. This operation allows excess energy on the grid to be captured and stored as elevated water.

We meet up with Phil at the pick-up point north of the reservoir.

Leslie looks at me. "That wasn't so bad. How far did we walk today?"

I check my GPS. "Ten miles."

Milene looks at Les. "Les, I've figured it out. We're 10-mile people. And yesterday, someone forced us to walk 12 miles."

After dinner, Phil and I drop Les and Milene back at their vehicle. Later, Les told me that they stopped on the way home at a fast-food place. When they got back in the car, Milene couldn't find her sunglasses, so she staggered back inside to look for them. While she was inside, Leslie pulled down the visor and looked in the mirror. She had her own sunglasses perched on top of her head and Milene's settled on her nose.

Segment 5

May 14–20 and June 3
Ludington to Suttons Bay
105 miles in 7 days

Total Trek Mileage: 355 miles

The BIG pack

Phil drives me to Ludington State Park to start the next leg of the journey. I pull out my pack from the trunk of the car. It is much larger and heavier than my over-the-shoulder sling pack. For part of this leg, I plan to camp, so my hammock/tent, extra clothes, and food are all jammed into my seriously outdoorsy pack. I hoist it onto my back and adjust the straps so most of the weight sits on my hips.

I wave goodbye to Phil and head up the shore.

It is a cool day, and the storm the previous night has left the lake churned and wild. Waves break high on the shore, occasionally forcing me to skip out of their reach and onto the softer sand. The lake works its magic on me in that first mile. Reinvigorated, I snap a perfect walking stick off a large piece of driftwood and am soon walking at a nice clip toward the Big Sable Lighthouse.

Thirty minutes into the day's walk, I reach back for my water bottle to find an empty carabiner clip. The plastic ring on the bottle must have fractured when I was jumping over driftwood, and I didn't hear it fall off because of the pounding waves.

This bottle had a filtering system allowing me to drink Lake Michigan water. I thought it was both symbolic and essential to be hydrated by the very body of water I was exploring. Not only was I walking its edge for 1,000 miles, but it was also inside me, its molecules becoming part of me.

The bottle had performed wonderfully to this point, only to abandon me now on the shores of Ludington State Park. I double-back, retracing my steps, hoping to find the bottle nestled safely in the crook of a driftwood log. After walking back more than a mile, I worry that it has been swept out into the lake. I consider drinking directly from the lake, but think about the parasite *giardia lamblia.* My son, Lucas, had gotten this intestinal parasite when he was three years old. I often took my boys to a stream to catch crayfish and find cool rocks when they were little. One day, I was looking at something that Ben had found and I glanced at Lucas just five feet away. He was lifting the plastic cup that we used to catch crayfish up to his mouth. I yelled, "Noooooooo!" splashed over to him, and swatted the cup from his lips, but he had already swallowed.

It is said of *giardia lamblia:* it won't kill you, but you'll wish that it would. Let's just say that "intestinal upset ensues" in a way that redefines the phrase. I'd seen what this little parasite could do and didn't want to risk it.

I call Phil and catch him before he is too far on his return drive home. He swings back and drives me to Ludington to look for a replacement bottle. We have no luck there, but hear about an outfitter store in Manistee.

There, they suggest we try Traverse City. By this time, my day is shot and there is no way I can walk the remaining miles between Ludington and Manistee, so we drive to Traverse City to buy a new bottle. On a whim, I also purchase some hand warmers that activate when exposed to air. Phil then drops me at Manistee to stay the night before resuming the trek the next day.

I tell myself to remain flexible with the trek, to roll with the challenges along the way, but it is difficult to lose a day like this.

The next morning, I feel less out-of-sorts about the delay and hit the lakeshore on the north side of the Manistee River. Along the first stretch of beach I see dozens of crayfish, some on the beach and others congregating in the shallows. These crustaceans are filter feeders, so where they thrive the water is quite clean. Indeed, the beaches and water along this stretch seem pristine.

I also see my first dead round goby on the beach. It was strange to see a species from so far away that was now thriving in the lake, and I'm sure it was even stranger from the fish's point of view to be transported halfway across the world and dumped into a completely different ecosystem.

When I reach the channel where Portage Lake drains into Lake Michigan, I climb onto the retaining wall and look into the water. It is crystal clear. I can see every detail of the rocks down for many feet. Nearby, there is a sleek red bass-boat with two fishermen working their lures near the rocks.

"Any luck?" I call over to them. The two men are dressed almost identically in jeans, sweatshirts, sunglasses, and black baseball caps.

"Nothing yet," the younger guy answers. "We just got out here."

"I was wondering if you guys would give me a ride across the channel? You'll save me from walking around the lake." I point inland to Portage Lake.

They look at me a moment, and my pack. The older guy looks at the retaining wall and the rocks, and then says, "Sure." He reels in his line and the other guy follows his lead. I shrug off my pack and descend the ladder a few rungs as they maneuver my way.

The boat looks like it had come directly out of the showroom, so I know they are concerned about bumping the rocks or the wall. I use my foot to steady the boat to keep it from hitting anything.

"Careful," the younger guy says. I swing my pack down to him. I can see his surprise at the weight. "Wow. How far you going with this?"

"I'm hiking up to Suttons Bay over the next week, but I've been hiking all the way around Lake Michigan since March." I step onto the boat and push off the ladder so we drift away from the wall. "You guys have the perfect day for fishing."

"Yeah," the younger guy says. "We teach at the same school and had the day off."

"Where do you teach?"

"Down in Muskegon," the older guy answers. "I teach history, he teaches science."

"I appreciate this. Thanks." It takes about a minute to cross the channel; the walk would have been at least two hours inland. We near the ladder on the far side, and I climb onto it while again keeping the boat from bumping the retaining wall, and loft my pack up onto the top of the wall.

"Thanks again, guys," I say as I climb the wall, and they push off, giving a final wave, and take up their fishing poles once again.

Bobcat, dead deer, and cougars, OH MY!

North of Portage Lake, it soon gets rather remote and the shoreline becomes rugged with high, wooded dunes flanking me to my right, with the expanse of calm lake to my left. There are miles without any signs of civilization, and I pass curious tracks along a small stream that look like a bobcat made them. Not a mile from the stream, a severed foreleg of a deer rests, bloody, on the shore.

A bobcat couldn't take down a full-sized deer. To forestall the obvious conclusion that something even larger had killed it, I think up a "Clumsy Deer Scenario" where the deer trips, conks its head on a rock, and is eaten by the bobcat.

Oh, clumsy, clumsy deer!

Then I think about all the times that I have stumbled on the trek so far, over icy rocks, through roots grabbing at my feet, over piles of driftwood. I begin to feel little ravenous cat eyes on me, waiting for me to blunder, stumble, and conk my head. At home, I have a 15-pound housecat who has some rather feral moments, so I am sure I can fend off a bobcat – as long as I have my walking stick and my wits about me.

To allay my fears, though, I yell, "Venison is DELICIOUS!"

There are wild cats bigger than bobcats in Michigan: cougars. And I don't mean the Demi Moore type. These big carnivores – over 100 pounds – have been seen all over the state. Cougars are genetically programmed to jump on the back of their prey and clamp their jaws on the neck, working their incisors between the vertebrae to sever the spinal cord so their prey will stop struggling. Then: dinnertime.

My main consolation was that I'd probably not see a cougar come at me. It would be over before I had time to say, "Venison is DELICIOUS!"

I hope that my larger pack would protect me, or somehow make me seem less of an option for a cougar dinner.

Or, maybe, the cougar would knock me over, pack and all, but I'd have time to pull out my pepper spray and spray the cat and not myself.

And I wished for a big cat that did not think pepper spray would make me taste even more delicious.

Ha-ha-ha-ha-ha

South of the town of Arcadia, I headed inland and hiked a stretch over high rolling dunes. After 16 miles of beach walking with my heavy pack, I was pretty done in for the day, but I pushed my way over the sandy dunes and out to roads that took me to the Arcadia House B&B.

When I got to my room, I sloughed off the pack and felt my shoulders magically rise. I stretched out on the bed and closed my eyes. I had done 17 miles with the heavy pack, and it took a larger toll on me than the lighter pack. I should have seen this coming. After forcing myself to eat dinner and feeling a bit dizzy afterward, I realized that I was probably fighting off a mild flu. I slept long and hard that night. In the morning, I pulled out my maps and realized I had planned to hike 25 miles that day.

Ha-ha-ha-ha.

At home, it was easy to look at maps and think, Well, I've done 24-mile days, so 25 won't be bad. But, I would have mostly forgotten about the pain, the limping, the exhaustion.

On top of that, almost any day I mapped out at home became a mile or two longer when measured by GPS. Twelve miles stretched to fifteen with an unforeseen diversion. Eighteen extended to twenty, if the shoreline was more irregular than maps had shown. On the ground, this 25-mile day could easily become 30, and with my heavy pack and strength level, I knew that there was little chance I'd make that distance.

Even if I miraculously did, I'd be a wreck the following day.

The wind had picked up overnight and was coming from the west, so I knew the lake would be pushing onto the shore again, probably forcing me to walk in the softer sand higher up. I decided to be realistic and split the one-day's hike into two.

This would take me to the city of Frankfort by evening, where I could rest up before camping the following night. I also opted to hike on Route 22 instead of the soft shore. Route 22 hugs the lake between Arcadia and Frankfort, so I could still see the lake most of the time and was even treated to some sweeping, scenic overlooks of the rising dunes and down into Frankfort Harbor.

It isn't an easy walk. The road rises and falls over 400 feet in places. But the trillium were in bloom with their happy, white petals which slowly turn to pink as they age.

I also saw little roadkill along the way, only two porcupines with poor timing.

Porcupines must have no muscle tone. Not that they need it. They have all those quills to protect them, but when a car hits them, they explode. It looks like a mob hit.

Yo, I want you to whack Spike. Do it in such a manner as to send a message.

Yikes!

I hiked a decent 12 miles into Frankfort, then dropped my pack and explored the quaint city a bit. After an early dinner, I crawled into bed and enjoyed it, because I knew the next night would be spent suspended between two trees.

The next day, I'd finally reach Sleeping Bear Dunes National Lakeshore.

Part of the attraction

I walked to the Frankfort harbor the next morning and hiked the shore to the Point Betsie Lighthouse. It is out in the middle of the lake, miles from here, that Lake Michigan reaches its maximum depth of over 900 feet.

Lake Michigan contains over a thousand cubic miles of water. Cubic MILES!

The Great Lakes are sometimes referred to as the "inland seas" or "America's Third Coast." Over the years, I'd heard many statistics about the Great Lakes. For instance: if you took all the water from the five lakes and spread it over the lower forty-eight states, it would cover to a depth of ten feet. Or how Lake Superior contains more water than the other four lakes combined. Even these statistics can't truly convey their vast size.

As I approached the lighthouse, I was beginning to get a sense of the scale of this lake, of its volume, width, length. With each step of this journey, with each wave that danced up on the sand near me, I became more intimate with this living mass of water.

The Point Betsie lighthouse is attached to a house – a white, barn-like structure topped with a red roof. When visiting this or any Lake Michigan lighthouse, I always think about the time when people manned these structures, charged with keeping them lit, knowing that vessels on the lake relied on those beacons to navigate treacherous waters. North of this point is the

Manitou Passage, a stretch of water leading between the North and South Manitou Islands, and beyond, the shore of northwest Michigan.

In reading about all the shipwrecks on the lake, I learned that there are many in this passage. Fresh water can sometimes be more dangerous than salt water. Fresh water has physical properties that allow waves to be created more quickly and closer together, and for the troughs between them to be deeper than for salt water under the same conditions. The many broken and submerged vessels testify to the fact that the Great Lakes can be deadly.

I reached Point Betsie on a Sunday. Even though the lighthouse was closed there was a steady stream of vehicles stopping. People, mostly older couples, popped out of their cars, walked out onto the beach, snapped a few photos, then drove away. I sat in the sand out of the wind and ate a caramel apple that I had brought with me from Frankfort.

This seemed like the perfect snack for the trek, sweet and wet and refreshing. I waved at people passing by, and they treated me as part of the attraction.

Sleeping Bear Dunes National Lakeshore

Soon after my break at Point Betsie, I entered the first section of the Sleeping Bear Dunes National Lakeshore. This park preserves about 35 miles of pristine shoreline, along with the North and South Manitou Islands. This segment of my Lake Trek, I know, would have some of my favorite parts of Michigan: the National Lakeshore and Leelanau Peninsula.

I pressed on to a trail that would take me inland to the Platte River Campground. The trail climbed over high, rolling dunes with patchy areas of low scrub grasses and shrubs. In one area of open sand on the dune face, I encountered a ghost forest. The spectral skeletons are the sun-bleached remains of trees, first entombed by the living dune, then revealed again when the winds shifted, migrating the sand away from the dead trees. Some of the ghost trees had been so exposed that they had toppled over, and their spiky stumps – which once reached down into the sand for water – now clawed at the air.

I startle several deer and they high-hurdle their way through the forest, flashing white tails at me. At the campground, I find the ranger station and lean my walking stick against the side of the building, then pull at the door.

It is locked. I unclip the hip belt, shrug off my pack and lean it near my stick. Then, I limp over to the map of the campground. As I'm trying to figure out which site to choose, the door of the station rattles open.

"I thought you were closed," I say.

"We always open for hikers," The ranger answers. She holds the door, and I drag my pack inside.

"Hiking around the park?" she asks as she slips behind the counter.

"Around the lake."

"Loon Lake?"

I laugh. "Michigan. Lake Michigan."

"Seriously?"

I nod. "I started in Chicago. I've done it in chunks, not all at once."

"Wow. You hiked through all that industry? The steel mills?"

"Not my favorite part. But I love this part of the lake. You picked a great spot to be a ranger." I look at the literature on the counter, gauging the weight of each piece, wondering which would be worthwhile to carry another fifty miles or so. Lifting a thin newspaper about the park, I think it's light enough to come along and I slip it into my pack.

"I do love it here," she says. "Kind of quiet now, but it will get busy soon enough. So. How long are you staying?"

We discuss the secluded sites nearest the lake, and I choose the one she recommends. We chat a bit longer, then I shoulder my pack and say good-bye. As I'm walking out the door, she calls to me. "Wait. I should probably tell you about this guy that's around sometimes."

She waves me into the back office. I follow her, and she points to a black-and-white photo of a scowling guy around 60 years old. "He's assaulted women in the park before. It's probably too early for him to be around, but that's what he looks like."

"Can't they lock him up?" I ask as I study his creepy face.

"He was banned from the park for two years, but that time's up." We look at his face together.

"He really looks like that," she adds. "He scowls like that all the time. I thought I should tell you."

"I always walk with a stick," I say, "so don't worry." She walks me out of the ranger station and watches me hike down the path.

"I wish I was coming with you," she shouts after me. I lift my walking stick and wave back to her.

By the time the sun sets, I have camp set up and a good fire crackling in the fire ring, with a decent pile of wood stacked nearby. The ranger had mentioned that it was going to get cold this night, so I unpack my hand warmers. *I'll use them if I have to,* I bravely think as I don my set of long underwear, followed by a few more layers from my pack. With all the clothes on, it is difficult to put my arms down at my sides, but I do feel toasty warm, especially by the fire.

I keep checking underneath my clothes to make sure I am not sweating. Sweat plus cold (as anyone who has watched those survival shows knows) equals hypothermia. I add layers as it cools down and don't sit too close to the fire.

As the sun sets, a raccoon emerges sleepily from a hollow tree nearby and sits there grooming himself.

"Nice you could join us," I taunt him.

He is unfazed by my mocking. I had already suspended my food in a tree, so I'm not worried about him. Fatigue takes over as the sunlight dims, so I let the fire die, spread the coals in the fire ring, and get into my tent/hammock and into my emergency blanket/sleeping bag.

I like gear that has slashes in the name. It denotes multiple uses, versatility, and thoughtful design. I hate sleeping on the ground, so I had packed a tent/hammock that suspends me between two trees. Then, I figured an emergency blanket fashioned into a sleeping bag should be delightfully warm, especially when paired with a lightweight travel blanket. I hadn't wanted to carry a standard sleeping bag because of the weight and bulk. I snuggle into my sleeping set-up after hanging my hand warmers in the pouch above my head (just in case). I soon fall into a deep I've-been-hiking-for-days coma/sleep.

I awaken in the dead of night because my hammock/tent is violently shaking. Bear attack? Monsoon? Creepy Guy? I panic. Then, noticing that there weren't any bear or creepy guy sounds and there isn't any wind – not even a gentle breeze – I realize that I have been awakened by my own violent shivering.

The raccoon is crashing around on the picnic table three feet away.

I ball up and rub my legs and arms with my gloved hands for a time, then I remember the hand warmers! I rip open two of them, shake them violently – not difficult since I'm still shivering – and work them into place between my layered clothing. I had plenty of layers on, so I'm not worried about getting too hot. It would be delightful, I think as I curl back into a heat-conserving ball, if indeed the warmers put out a lot of heat. Too hot sounded nice.

What isn't delightful is the fact that my emergency blanket/sleeping bag is excellent at holding in moisture. It is moist to the touch on the inside, and my blanket is beginning to get clammy. Wet plus cold is bad, but I don't have too many options at this point other than to wait for sunrise. I reposition my hat and my hood and cram my hands in my now-warm armpits and try to doze off.

I can hear the raccoon noisily climbing the tree where my pack hangs.

Unfortunately, just as I begin to warm up, I realize that all the shivering made it rather imminent that I go pee. The last thing I wanted to do was to leave the fetal position, but there was no putting it off.

I extricate myself from my sleeping set-up and tumble out of the hammock and run to a group of trees. When I return, I take a moment to do some jumping jacks. My breath forms fleeting fog in the cold, crisp night. I notice that I can see fairly well, even in the dense darkness, and I look up. The night sky is alight with stars. The Milky Way is a cloud of light, distinct and enormous. I can perceive various shades of grays and blacks since my eyes have had time to switch over to fully using the rods in my retina.

The wondrous night sky elates me. I spread my arms and rotate in a slow circle attempting to take in the cosmos.

Then, exhausted and freezing, I climb back into my hammock/tent and wiggle into my sleeping sack.

The rest of the night is an icy, noisy hell. There are at least two kinds of owls who call to other owls to tell them important owl news. Deer crash around. Coyote howl and run to another spot where they howl some more.

The raccoon keeps at it, too, climbing and crashing. He couldn't have been louder if he had been banging pots and pans together. At one point, he may have even located a couple to do just that. It was like the nature channel, in surround sound, full volume.

At the coldest part of the night, I devise an intricate plot to knock out the raccoon and wear him as a warm hat. By the time the birds start singing at dawn, I am exhausted and chilled and keep squinting through the mesh to see when the sun would reach a high-enough angle to illuminate and warm my hammock/tent.

At the moment, this whole camping part of the adventure seemed slightly insane.

After packing camp, I watch the raccoon sleepily (and almost silently) climb to its den and crawl in for a good day's sleep. I call him several very bad names that I hope translate richly in raccoon language. Then, I heave my pack up onto my sore shoulders and limp back to the lake. It feels good to be heading back to the lakeshore, leaving the cacophony of the woods behind me.

The smell of the predator

I begin hiking the length of Platte Bay, 9 miles to the city of Empire. Much of the way I hike on rolling, dune-grass-sprouting sand because the wind is once again pushing the lake up onto the flat part of the shore. High, wooded dunes hug the shore to my right, and I feel surrounded by wilderness, isolated from civilization.

I think back to a time when I stayed at a rustic cabin in this part of Michigan several years back. I had gotten up early and had stepped out into the cold, November morning. Something large was moving off into the woods and I saw bear tracks and a pile of scat so fresh it was steaming in the cold, morning air. An intense, musky smell slowly dissipated. Bear smell. The smell of the predator.

I remember this smell as I hike this remote stretch of Platte Bay. The terrain gives plenty of cover for predators like cougar. The wind is in my face, so they could easily track me. I keep moving, glancing back over my shoulder to look for any movement on the face of the wooded dune. I pass the remains of a deer that is just a furry coat with four jumbled legs sticking out, like the deer was vacuumed head-first out of his hide. Not too far from that is another pile of deer bones and three smaller piles of fur.

I am strolling a prime hunting corridor. The wind shifts and that musky, wild smell – the smell of the predator – fills the air. I remember something about cougars being reluctant to attack the front of their prey (or was that only tigers?!), so I begin walking backward, scanning the hills for movement.

It is tough to walk the low, rolling dunes facing forward, and even tougher doing it backwards with a heavy pack. After stumbling twice, I turn and walk forward again. I figure it would not help my survival factor to fall down. That's probably the cougar equivalent of a dinner bell. I was sure now I had detected some movement on the dune face, but it is windy, so it's difficult to know if it was an animal or just the scrubby trees blowing in the wind.

As I turn to face forward, the musky smell grows stronger. I walk faster, pulling harder on my walking stick. My stick is sturdy enough to at least deflect a pouncing cougar, I figure, so I grip it tightly and plan how to spin and strike the killer cat. I tighten the straps on my pack as I hurry along, cinching it higher up on my shoulders to give some protection to my vulnerable and tasty neck.

The wind swirls again and the musky smell surrounds me. Sweat drips off my face and – not breaking my fast stride – I lift my arm across my face and wipe the sweat onto my sleeve.

The smell grows even stronger.

I pull out my pepper spray. I push myself into a slow jog on the rolling dunes. I wipe the sweat again onto my shirt, and happen to smell my shirt as my arm crosses my face.

That pungent, feral, musky smell surrounds me now because it *is* me. All this rushing, fearful hiking, on top of a night sleeping in my clothes, has made *me* the one who smells like a wild animal.

I slow down and stow my pepper spray.

By the time I get to Empire, I am done for the day. Between the frozen night without much sleep and the exciting hike, those 9 miles felt like 29. I catch a ride into Glen Arbor with a sympathetic guy returning from kayaking on the lake.

I find the Sylvan Inn B&B, get under a quilt, and elevate my sore feet. On the news, I hear that the previous night's low temperature was below freezing.

My blisters had gotten deeper and evolved into blood blisters. I had never had this happen before. I thought back to other times I had blisters. A trick we used on my high school basketball team was to wrap blisters with white, cloth athletic tape. It acted like a second skin, reducing friction. I limped over to a grocery store, bought food for dinner and a roll of white tape for my feet.

I tried to be realistic about the camping option. My days available for this Lake Trek were limited. If I only did 10 miles a day (and not the 15 I'd been averaging), then I could probably camp and still function the next day. But if I only did 10 miles a day, that would stretch the timetable of the trek out longer, take me away from home for longer stretches, and possibly compromise my ability to reflect on the experience, to write my notes in the evening, because of fatigue and the extra work of camping (and running from wild animals when I was delusional).

I realized I had not undertaken the trek as a wilderness survival experiment. I enjoyed the shore and the waves, the rocks and sand and bluffs. I also enjoyed the towns, and meeting the people who lived near the lakeshore.

Besides, all the setting up and cooking and cleaning and packing away reminded me too much of housekeeping. The trek was supposed to take me away from that and let me experience the lake.

Quite honestly, after hiking 15-20 miles, I liked a hot shower and a meal someone else cooked. And I adored a comfy bed.

I enjoyed moving faster with a lighter pack. And I liked being warm at night instead of plotting to wear a concussed raccoon as a hat.

The hand of the glaciers

Sleeping Bear Dunes National Lakeshore is divided into three sections. I had just walked the first section from near Point Betsie to the town of Empire. The middle section is shorter, stretching from Empire, around Sleeping Bear Point, to Glen Arbor. This was the section I knew best from previous visits to the area. The Pierce Stocking Scenic Drive, Dune Climb, and Maritime Museum are in this section. Some of the tallest dunes on the lake are here, over 450 feet high above the lake.

This was the area I had gotten a ride through, but I opted to not hike the missed shoreline since I had covered most of it before.

The third section of the park's shoreline was ahead, the stretch from Glen Arbor to the east side of Good Harbor Bay. I walked the few blocks east through Glen Arbor. Anytime I glanced up a side street to the left, Lake Michigan was right there at the end of the block. It must be delightful to live where the lake is so close at hand.

Glen Lake is near the city. It's shaped like two conjoined lakes. This is an orphan body of water, originally part of Lake Michigan, but with its connecting channel filled in over time by blowing sand.

The hand of the glaciers is easy to recognize in this region with its massive features and obvious moraines. Estimates of the glaciers' size (there were four waves of glaciers that gouged out the Great Lakes during the Ice Age) put them between one to two *miles* tall. I read one scientific study that was able to measure the rate at which the shoreline was still "bouncing back" from the weight of the glaciers over 10,000 years ago.

When they finally melted, the glaciers dropped all of the rocks and sand and clay they were carrying. Perched dunes and beach dunes abound here. A perched dune forms when the glacial moraine – the rocks and gravel pushed in front of a moving glacier – is then covered over with blown sand. The wave action of the lake then cuts away at the headland, leaving a rather dramatic dune feature that sits high above the shore on a plateau. Both Sleeping Bear Dune and the dune at Pyramid Point are perched dunes.

Perched dunes have the disquieting habit of occasionally "sloughing off" large chunks into the lake. The waves slowly erode the edges of these dunes, periodically causing it to become unstable. There are reports of several acres of the top of the dune occasionally disappearing, and the resultant landslide can reach up to two miles out along the bottom of the lake.

When I reach Good Harbor Bay, there is a pleasant breeze. Gentle waves pulse over the shallows, wetting the band of colorful pebbles there. Further out from shore, the water is a milky turquoise blue; the waves are keeping sediment suspended in the water. In the distance, the water is banded in deeper and deeper shades of blue until – where the lake floor drops off to a great depth – it is midnight blue stretching to the horizon.

As I hike at the top of the frothing waves on the sand scattered with stones, I think how odd it is that I have not found a Petoskey stone yet. Then I look down and see three of them clustered together near my boot. It's rare to see two at a time, let alone three.

These stones are the fossilized remains of an ancient coral that thrived in the shallow sea that covered this land in the Devonian Period, millions of years pre-dinosaur. The ancient coral is called *hexagonaria percarinatae,* and it grew in colonies of neatly ordered, six-sided corals all pressed together. It has a distinctive honeycomb pattern, and its fossilized remains are an unmistakable find.

Since these three Petoskey stones at my feet are on National Lakeshore

Park land, I leave them grouped there for others to marvel at, if they happen to look down at the right moment.

I've always been a rock hound. The windowsill in my home office and the edges of my desk are lined with rocks from my travels. There is purple granite from the Rockies, slate fractured by an earthquake in Alaska, a smooth, chicken-bone-shaped rock from France. Flat containers display more rocks from many visits to the shore of Lake Michigan.

Holding any of these stones takes me back to the place it was found. There is something about smoothing a stone in my hand, rolling it around, polishing it, that connects me to the earth once again. I've found that by rubbing these stones with a cream made to keep cuticles soft, they stay bright and polished – like they just emerged from the water – for several months. When they dull, I polish them again, taking time to rediscover the qualities of each stone and why I gathered it in the first place.

It was torturous for me to hike the shoreline and not pick up handfuls of rocks, but adding any weight to my backpack was a strong deterrent. I resolved to only pick up smaller specimens – until the last few hours of a segment where I could be less restrictive about how many ounces-accumu-lating-into-pounds of rocks I gathered.

I hiked to the end of the park along the bay, then cut inland to Route 22 and headed north along the lake to the city of Leland. I felt like I had regained my strength and my stride. And the athletic tape I bought in Glen Arbor seemed to be doing the trick with the epic blisters on my heels.

I hiked 21 miles that day including the mile into Leland and back to my hotel. Looking at my maps that night, I reluctantly realized that to hike to the tip of the Leelanau Peninsula to the city of Northport, then back down to Suttons Bay was too long for one day's hike, so I decided to cut across the Leelanau Peninsula.

The last day of this segment was hot, so I was sad to be leaving the lakeshore with the cooling breeze and cold water. By noon, the day had reached 86 degrees. I soaked a towel in cool water and tied it around my neck to keep my brain cool. This segment was one of extremes. My strength fluctuated as did the weather and terrain. I was exhausted from the heat by the time I reached Suttons Bay, and – thankfully for the other patrons – I find a café with outdoor seating, a spot where I could cool down and dry off in the shade of a maple tree.

Afterward, I hiked the last few miles to the pick-up point for the end of this segment, a place called Black Star Farms.

Wine country

The 45th parallel cuts across the Leelanau Peninsula. Around the globe, any spot on this line point is exactly halfway between the equator and North Pole. On it, you are at the same latitude as some of the finest wine country in the world: the Bordeaux in France and Italy's Piedmont region.

I had walked past many vineyards on the Leelanau Peninsula (there are over 800 acres of vines thriving there) and now was greeted with a curving, terraced vineyard at the entry to Black Star Farms. After walking in the heat, I was ecstatic to slip into the cool jacuzzi bathtub in my room. When I had recovered a bit, I met up with Phil and we walked the grounds of the farm.

Black Star Farms is idyllic. There are horses in corrals near the inn that like to have their noses rubbed. There is a market on the grounds where farmers sell their fresh produce. They also have a cheese-making operation, including a cool cave where the cheeses are aged.

Then, there's the tasting room. This area is known for its award-winning white wines – Rieslings and pinot blancs especially – but some of the reds here are fantastic, too. Black Star has also branched out into fruit-infused spirits and even a maple dessert wine. Phil and I tasted our way through the selections and enjoyed the cheese made on site. I was ready to move in to the inn forever. After the sumptuous farm-to-table breakfast the next day, I was almost weeping that I had to leave.

Backtracking to cover missed miles

On the third of June, I headed back to the lake to cover the missed miles from the first day of this segment. My mom and Phil drove me up to Manistee and explored the lakeside towns while I hiked south to Ludington.

It felt wrong to have the lake on my right side. For one thing, all of the tendons and ligaments in my legs and feet had to adjust to the slant going the other way. I was, according to the strict vision of the trek, going backwards. Why should that matter? And why was I so determined to cover these few, missing miles?

There was something important to me about completely encircling the lake with my trek, to connecting the segments, to not leaving huge gaps. That completion was part of the quest and important, I thought, to being faithful to the spirit of the Lake Trek. I wasn't just out strolling the groomed beaches on the lake, but was exploring its edge on a long, intimate, ever-connected arc.

I was convinced this grand circle would yield some understanding, some greater knowledge, and possibly something less tangible.

I was becoming attuned to the rhythms of the lake, the connections of rivers and streams to the big body of water, sensitized to the flow of air over waves. I was also connecting to the shoreline, the undulations, the geology, the plants and wildlife. The shapes of the shoreline were meaningful; for instance, I knew a certain curve would allow a river to merge with the lake, while a larger curve would create a bay, creating a space that would calm the waters enough to allow more plant life to thrive.

I felt like I belonged, that I was part of the circle, that I was there to record the lake in my body with each stride.

I had a sunny day to cover these miles; the lake pulsed gentle waves. There was sandy beach to walk for the majority of the day, with only one long stretch where a series of decaying, wooden seawalls buttressed the flanks of the dunes. I weaved in and out of these with the waves, sometimes was forced to climb up and over them when the lake splashed up against the wall. While hiking one of the rolling dunes, I almost stepped on a sleeping fawn nestled in a shallow depression partially covered by dune grass. We scared each other, and the fawn jumped up and bounded away.

As the sun drifted across the sky, the angle of its rays made the water come alive and sparkle. I watched a lake freighter make its way across the horizon on the silver-flecked inland sea. The beach widened as I approached the curve north of Big Sable Lighthouse, and the lighthouse appeared in the distance, tall with white and black bands.

I finished the last of this segment at the entry to the state park where my mom and Phil waited for me. My mom got out of the car and walked over to me.

"Good day?" she asked.

"Yep. 18 miles."

She turned and walked at my side for the last 100 yards. When we reached the car, she chuckled and said, "Now I can say I walked with you!"

I jumped in the car, and they took me out to a great dinner at the Blu Moon Café in Ludington.

When I got home that evening, I wondered why all of the chairs at my house felt different. They seemed to have gotten hard and uncomfortable. Then I realized that it was my butt that had changed. After over 350 miles of hiking on sand and dunes and roads and rock, my backside had notice-ably firmed and toned.

Segment 6

June 8–16
Suttons Bay to Mackinaw City
147 Miles in 9 days

Total Trek Mileage: 502 miles

Inland Seas Education Center

Before I began hiking the next segment, the final stretch of Michigan's Lower Peninsula leading up to the Straits of Mackinac, Phil and I stopped in the city of Suttons Bay. I wanted to visit the Inland Seas Education Center there. This organization has a building with offices and exhibits, but the heart of the center is tied to a nearby dock. It is a sailboat, a teaching vessel designed to take groups of children out onto the lake, a classroom afloat on the bay.

We enter the center and poke around the displays a bit. There are many large fish tanks teeming with lake life, and, nearby, a life-size model of the sea lamprey. This snakelike fish has a round mouth lined with sharp teeth it uses to latch onto a host fish. I've seen photos of large salmon with multiple round wounds from the lamprey. They can suck the life from even the largest salmon.

Recently, scientists have isolated and synthesized a lamprey phero-mone, the chemical signal the male secrets to attract females so that little lamprey can be produced. Scientists are using it to lure lamprey into traps. Early tests prove it attracts both female and male; it's a "lamprey party time" message.

I pick up the lamprey model and look at Phil. "Take a picture," I say. I look horrified and hold it so it looks like it's attached to my face.

Phil laughs and snaps a photo. "Now, you attacking it," he suggests. I hold it up like I'm sucking on its side for the second photo.

There is a large display about the invasive zebra mussel. A bicycle extracted from the bay is suspended from the ceiling above tanks filled with live zebra mussels. The bike is completely encrusted with their shells, as if someone with a glue gun and a crafting mania went wild decorating it with little striped shells.

I wander back to the office area and track down Tom Kelly, the director of the center. He had emailed me about their work, inviting me to go out on the bay in their boat.

"Come in," Tom ushers us into his office and moves large stacks of folders from chairs to the floor so we can sit. Tom has graying hair and a salt-and-pepper beard. He looks like he'd be at home at the wheel of a triple-masted schooner.

"How's your hike going?"

"Fantastic," I say. "I've walked from Chicago to your office," I smile. "I'm impressed by your zebra mussel display."

"Those little guys have really changed the bay." He is referring to Grand Traverse Bay, that scoop of water north of Traverse City. "We've seen the water clarity go way up since they colonized here."

"How long have you been taking measurements in the bay?"

"Twenty years now. But one of the measurements most important to us is that we've taken over 80,000 kids out on the water. Not only do they have the experience of sailing, they also interact with the lake in a hands-on, scientific way. For the lakes to stay healthy, it's got to matter – not only to us, but to these kids and their kids."

"I couldn't agree more."

"Let me show you our boat," he says, springing up from his chair. He grabs a rubberized rain slicker from a hook and slips into it.

It is drizzling as we make our way through the puddles to the dock. "Sorry it's not a good day for a sail."

"I'll take you up on that next time I visit," I say thinking about the miles I still have to walk today down the bay to Traverse City.

The wooden sailboat is seventy-seven feet long, painted green and white. Tom springs over the gap between the dock and boat, then plunges down into the hold. Phil and I try to not fall into the bay as we follow.

The hold is designed around a small laboratory. Narrow, bunked births line the inside of the hull; sometimes they take groups out on the water for longer trips. A typical class day-trip would include touring the center's educational exhibits, then going out on the boat into Grand Traverse Bay. There, the kids take samples of the water and lake life. They perform scientific measurements like pH, water clarity, temperature, dissolved oxygen, phosphate and nitrate levels. They can also view plankton through a microscope, study sediment and lake plants, and catch fish and other organisms living in the lake. The data that the kids have gathered has charted two decades of changes in the bay, including the increasing clarity since the zebra mussels took up residence in the Great Lakes.

One of the keys to restoring the lakes is to educate kids about the importance of this vast resource, to let them know it is a gift that needs our care. What better way to convey this than to have them experience the wind and waves of Lake Michigan, to pull up a bucket of water or bottom sediment, to peer into the secrets of the lake through the lens of a microscope?

I thank Tom for his important work, shoulder my pack, and walk south.

The heavens open

After 24 days on the Lake Trek, I had seen some wild wind and waves, and even some snow flurries, but very little rain. That changed this day. I walked south along Route 22 toward Traverse City in a steady rain. Low clouds hovered at what felt like the level of my forehead. The clouds stayed, but the rain tapered off after only an hour, and my rain gear kept me comfortable during the deluge.

The swish-swish-swish of my rain pants gave a new rhythm to my walking.

As always, I tried to keep as near the lake as possible, but along Grand Traverse Bay I had to stay on the shoulder of the nearest road for most of the way. The protected bay keeps the water calmer than on the open lake; this allows sediment to deposit along the shore, and water plants grow in these sheltered areas. And in this popular area, many houses are built near the water for this reason. If I tried to walk the waterline, I'd be crossing their very small backyards, and grasses growing out into the water effectively blurred that "public zone" I had been walking. I stuck to the roads and made my way to Traverse City.

Known at the Cherry Capital of the World, Traverse City nestles at the bottom of Grand Traverse Bay. The surrounding area grows the majority of the sour cherries produced in this country. The city is known as a great "foodie" city, too. Chefs take advantage of the abundance of local produce and create amazing farm-to-table fare. Phil and I had the best dinner at The Cooks' House, then I bought some handmade chocolates at Phil's on Front. We stayed at a lumber baron's mansion converted into a B&B – the Wellington Inn – and enjoyed roaming the ornate rooms filled with the city's history.

Then, the next day, I continued up the East Bay to Elk Rapids.

There is something oddly tiring about walking on the side of the road. I was always invigorated when walking by the lake, even if it was rocky or hilly, but walking on the roads left me exhausted by the end of the day.

Planting Fish

In Elk Rapids, I spotted a DNR tanker truck used to transport fingerling salmon from the hatcheries to the lake. The driver was just getting out of the cab. He stretched, and looked out on the water.

"Are you putting fish into the lake?" I asked.

"Nope. All the fish are planted for the year," he said.

That's what they call it. Planting fish. Like a crop.

We've planted millions of coho and Chinook in the lake. These are species native to the Pacific Ocean. The fish still have the instinct and ability to spawn, but most of the rivers where they lay their eggs are too silty for successful hatching of their eggs. So, each year, the DNR gathers eggs and sperm from mature salmon, grows them to fingerling size in several hatcheries around the Great Lakes, then releases them in the spring.

Okay, I'm going to say it: we have really screwed up the ecosystem of the lake. Fish like the lake herring, emerald shiners, yellow perch, walleye, whitefish and lake sturgeon used to co-exist in waters up to 150 feet deep. Deeper water species like chub, sculpin, and lake trout stayed further out in the lakes. The lake ecosystem was in balance.

When settlers displaced the Native tribes around the Great Lakes, everything was tossed out of balance. It began with the deforestation in the late 1800s, rolling all that lumber into the rivers to float the logs to mills. At its peak, the city of Muskegon alone had 50 sawmills operating simultaneously. Fifty! It was a wood-driven economy in the 1800s. Wood fed most steam-powered machines, including the boats on the lake. Wood was needed out on the plains to build shelters for the westward-bound settlers. Wood was needed in abundance after the Chicago Fire.

Wood was, simply, money.

The result? Deforesting the riverbanks removed the shade from the rivers, allowing the sun to warm the water. Species of trout and other fish that had spawned in these cool rivers for thousands of years still swam upstream, but the water in many rivers was too warm for their eggs to hatch, so their numbers diminished.

Then, people overfished the lakes. As early as the late 1800s there were reports that annual whitefish harvests declined by more than half over two decades. Sturgeon harvests fell even more drastically in the same span of time. Fishermen back then didn't realize that sturgeon don't even think about spawning until they are at least 20 years old. All those monster fish they pulled out of the lakes – sturgeon can grow up to 6 feet long and weigh 200 pounds – were the breeding stock of the species.

The giant freshwater mussel was harvested to extinction. They were gathered for their shells, which made lovely buttons, a multi-million dollar industry around the turn of the 20th century. When plastic buttons displaced shells, it was too late; by then the mussels were gone.

As manmade channels were dug to improve shipping in and out of the Great Lakes, invasive Atlantic species like the alewife (a small silver fish in the herring family) and sea lamprey made their way in. The lamprey killed off the fish at the top of the food chain. This in turn allowed the alewife population to explode.

At one time, it is estimated that 90% of the fish biomass in the lakes consisted of alewives. Unfortunately, these little fish can't deal with the lake warming as quickly as it does after the winter, so they often have mass dieoffs in the spring. Back in the 1970s, bulldozers and dump trucks worked the beaches to scrape up and haul away the tons of little silver carcasses.

And the smell! Rotting fish. For miles along the lakeshore.

The solution? Enter the current practice of stocking the lake with salmon native to the Pacific, to feed on the alewives.

Many other invasive species have taken up residence in the lakes. The round goby – along with many other species – were brought here in ballast water. The round goby feed on almost anything. People all around the lake spoke of years past when they would catch a stringer of perch in an afternoon. Now they caught mostly round goby, if they caught anything at all.

When I started this trek, I crossed bridges over shipping canals south of Chicago that connect Lake Michigan to the Mississippi River system. Guess what? This is another entry point for invasive species. The Asian carp that has taken over the Mississippi River is now making its way toward Lake Michigan's waters. The Army Corps of Engineers has installed two electric barriers in the canals, but at least one carp has gotten past them. These fish are voracious eaters, can grow to be 100 pounds, and spawn three times a year. They would quickly dominate the ecosystem in the Great Lakes, devastating the sport fishing industry.

In short, we've screwed it up. The Great Lakes have a largely orchestrated, man-controlled ecosystem at this point. If the Asian carp enter the lakes, it will all be thrown out-of-whack once again.

Miss Sadie and the Cowboy

North of Elk Rapids, I was finally able to return to the shoreline. There were still areas of wetlands, but there often was a ribbon of sand through the wetter areas for me to walk.

Healthy wetlands are good for the lake. They filter the water, offer havens for young lake life and shelters for wildlife. I saw schools of small fish and tadpoles, many birds, and even a very fat, black snake in these areas.

There is only one venomous snake in Michigan, the Massasauga rattler. They are rare, listed as a "species of special concern" due to their dwindling numbers. I thought the snake I saw was a rat snake, but later learned that rat snakes probably don't live that far north. I double-checked details about the Massasauga; turns out it can be almost completely black at times and that it loves to live in these coastal swales and marshes. So that may have been what I spotted. In any event, we startled each other equally, and it streaked off into the bushes.

I also saw my first bald eagle of the trek here. A powerful bird of prey, it flew parallel to the shore, clutching a large salmon in its talons.

A local woman, Gerry, who had been following my adventure contacted me; she wondered if she could walk with me. We met up north of Elk Rapids.

Gerry had moved from Southeast Michigan up here to Antrim County, a place she had fallen in love with over the years. Antrim County was named for a district of the same name in Ireland. Before that, its name was Meegisee, the Ojibwe word for eagle.

She is a happy woman, brimming with facts and history about the area. Her dogs, a terrier named Miss Sadie and a cocker spaniel named the Cowboy, also joined us. Like any dogs I'd seen on the beach, they were having the time of their lives. Gerry took an interesting approach to the leash law: she had each dog on a leash, then looped the leashes together so the dogs "walked" each other. They kept out of trouble by sticking together.

The waterfowl seemed to congregate and pose for us as we walked. Gulls perched on rocks offshore while several swans glided by. Pintail ducks gathered their large broods of chicks and scooted out into the bay together. The water was shallow quite a way out from the shore, and blooms of the algae *cladophora* lay in the shallows and in patchy heaps up on land.

"When it warms up," Gerry said as we walked over a clump of the algae, "this stuff rots and stinks something awful."

"Is this an invasive species?" I asked.

"No, it's native, but it's been growing out of control the last few years."

"That's *fragmites,*" I said, pointing to a tall patch of grass on the shoreline. "That's invasive, and I hear it's almost impossible to get rid of."

"I've seen more and more of that along here lately." Gerry knew her wild flowers. She pointed out the bright-yellow marsh marigold, also called cowslip.

Gerry and her canine companions couldn't stay with me for long; she had to get to work and the dogs looked like they had earned their afternoon nap. Before leaving, she told me about the large deposit of Antrim shale that I would find farther north, near the town of Norwood. She said that the Native Americans used to go there to gather stones for their arrowheads and tools.

As I walked north along the east side of the bay, I could see both the Old Mission Peninsula, a thin strip of land that juts into the middle of Grand Traverse Bay, and, behind it, the Leelanau Peninsula across the calm water. Both of these tips of land have historic lighthouses on them, which long ago guided boats past the shallows and into the safety of the bay.

I had once spent a week as a volunteer keeper at the Grand Traverse Lighthouse. It was in November, so much of our work was getting the buildings battened down for the harsh winter. We put boards up over windows, wrapped tarps around stone planters, and decorated the lighthouse for the holiday season visitors. Thankfully, we could enjoy the November evenings relaxing and reading with electric lights. In the pre-electric days, the keeper and his family used kerosene lamps, and for the strong, lens-focused light in the tower, the keeper had to carry oil up the stairs to fuel the flame that cast its saving light for sailors out on the dark waters.

The Grand Traverse Lighthouse was operational for over 100 years and was decommissioned in the 1970s. Instead, there is now an ugly, metal tower with a rotating beacon on the shore to guide navigation.

When I passed the level of the tip of the longer Leelanau Peninsula across the bay, the waves picked up since the shoreline was no longer sheltered. I was back on the open lake. The lakeshore transitioned from tumbled, colorful stones to sand. Then, near the town of Norwood, the sand was replaced by the scattered pieces of tumbled, gray shale that Gerry had mentioned. A massive outcropping flanks this stretch of shore; roundish stones so large I could barely encircle them with my arms sat in the shallow surf. They look like something the Flintstones would use for seating around their dinner table. These stones – called concretions – formed within the shale and are comprised of a type of calcite called anthraconite. As the shale fell away over thousands of freeze/thaw cycles, these massive stones popped out of the crumbling shale wall.

I had never seen any geology like this along the lake (and would not see it again during my trek). Along some stretches here, it looked like someone had paved the shoreline with black shale tiles. In other parts, like someone had scattered tens of thousands of palm-size pieces of shale, each irregular piece smoothed by the tumbling action of the waves. It looked like a massive puzzle box had been ripped open and the pieces scattered on the shore.

A small waterfall cascaded down a wall of the exposed, black rock. Along another stretch, grasses and mosses had grown out of pockets in the wall, softening the rock face with tendrils of green. Some chert was mixed into the shale wall. This is a form of quartz that fractures leaving sharp edges, so this may have been the stone that the Native Americans used for scrapers and arrowheads.

Along this stretch I saw more marsh marigold, this time blooming with the tiny blue forget-me-not flowers with their yellow centers. It looked as if nature had arranged a bouquet.

Not too far north of this unique geology, I entered Fisherman's Island State Park. The park is named after a small island that sits in the middle of its five miles of shoreline. A strip of land connected the island to the shore because the lake level, although up almost a foot this year, was still historically low. This park is a haven for wildlife. I slowed to watch the ducks and geese with their young, to stroll with some massive salmon plying the shallows, to spy on deer feeding on tender marsh plants.

Along a very remote stretch of this park, I saw some enormous tracks a ways off in the sand. *Huge dog,* I thought. Then, as the tracks came nearer, I thought, *someone should clip the long nails on that giant dog.* When I came upon a decaying log that had been ripped to shreds on the shoreline, I realized what it was: *wow, a bear did this.* A black bear had, indeed, walked this shoreline not too long before I did. I placed my hand in the sand next to the impressive footprint and took a photo. I straightened up and smelled the air, but I didn't detect anything nearby.

As I approached the north end of the park, I heard a distinct, deep thrumming that emanated from the cement company on the point west of the city of Charlevoix. I walked inland around the plant and quarry and into Charlevoix, over the bridge that spans the channel between Lake Charlevoix and Lake Michigan, then returned to the shore for a ways.

The beach past the channel had some of the most riotously colorful small stones – all tumbled smooth by the waves – that I had seen along the lake. Each handful was a gorgeous mixture of browns and reds and oranges and tans and blacks. This pleasant beach transitioned quickly into rocky wetlands, then into a large marshy area, so I had to turn inland once again.

The shoreline of Little Traverse Bay, which begins east of Charlevoix and ends north of Harbor Springs, is mostly inaccessible. It is quite rocky in areas, and the land often becomes elevated near the bay and drops off into the water. Some of this shoreline is owned by the power company and is restricted.

The more suitable option was to follow the Little Traverse Wheelway, a bike path that stretches 23 miles along the edge of the bay. I picked up this trail east of Charlevoix.

A college friend, Rick, joined me for part of the path. His family had always spent time in the Charlevoix area when he was growing up, and now his sister has a house there. She drove up in her large SUV and Rick jumped out wearing jeans and a sweatshirt over a polo shirt. I hugged him and greeted his sister.

"You won't need this," I said, tugging at his sweatshirt sleeve. It's a warm day, and I'm sweating in just a light t-shirt.

He look a little dubious, but tugs off the sweatshirt and tosses it to his sister. "Promise I'll survive this?" Rick is a dentist and not inclined to outdoor adventures.

"We're walking a bike path all day," I laughed as I straightened the collar on his crisp polo. "I'll take it easy on you. And if you pass out, I'll drag your body back to civilization."

We stroll for a couple miles, catching up on our lives. "When your sister told me about this I thought, 'That's just like Loreen!'"

"You weren't surprised at all?"

"I'm more surprised that I'm walking with you!"

I was glad to hear that enthusiasm about my trek was contagious.

As we passed East Park on the bay, we noticed that fences and NO TRESPASSING signs block off our access.

"People were scuba diving offshore here a few years back, and they got chemical burns from the water," Rick said.

He told me that a cement company used to be along this stretch of the bay, but the buildings had been torn down and buried on site. After testing the water, it was determined that liquid leaching from the site was at pH levels that could cause severe burns. Cement production facilities are also known to produce byproducts that can be high in mercury, arsenic, furans, and dioxins. The still fenced-off park was closed in 2006 just as it was completed.

As we approached the city of Petoskey, we have a high vantage point overlooking the city and the bay. Large rocks populated the shallows.

"Those rocks used to be covered with zebra mussels, but they've all died off here," Rick said.

"Because of the toxins in the water?" I asked.

"I guess so."

I have since learned that the city of Petoskey's wells are near the buried cement kiln, but, so far, tests have found them to be uncontaminated.

Rick walked with me a couple of miles out of Petoskey, then I continued alone to Petoskey State Park, on the eastern edge of the bay. Here, the strong wave action has created a long, sandy beach. At the beginning of this day the bay was like glass, but by the time I got to the beach, it was choppy from the wind.

I hiked most of this beach barefoot, my feet cooling in the waters of Little Traverse Bay. As I turned west, though, the shoreline got immediately marshy, so I headed slightly inland to a road that paralleled the bay into the lovely village of Harbor Springs.

Out of time

This segment was the longest, in both days and miles, that I had walked so far. It was around the seventh day that I noticed time blurring. What day of the week it was no longer mattered. All that existed was miles. Miles never shortened. They were a constant. When driving a car, one merely has to press the gas pedal to feel the miles shorten, but when one is walking, each step must be taken. Even if I ran for a bit, I might cover the miles in a shorter amount of time, but the steps were still mine, the sweat and energy expended were from within me.

It was also along this segment that I seemed to find a rhythm both within my body and with my movement through the land. I could begin the day, set off on the trek, and not have to negotiate anymore. There was no more bargaining, *make it two more miles and I'll pull out the chocolate.* I started hiking and could keep going pretty much all day. I had learned in the last segment to ignore the pain from my feet, and this helped tremendously.

The lack of negotiation with my body freed my mind up. I noticed smells more keenly: wildflowers, skunk cabbage, marshy decomposition, or the crisp, fresh air off the lake. And I could think the long, uninterrupted thought that is almost impossible in everyday life. I began to ponder the connections of the people to the lake, the economy to the lake, of invasive species, the cost of dumping sewage or industry byproducts into the lake versus dealing with them another way. I considered the complexity of the lake's ecosystem in all its intricacies.

Earlier in the trek, I had walked through the lakeshore of Grand Haven, Michigan, along the Grand River. It is into this river that the city of Grand Rapids used to routinely – during large rainstorms – dump its sewage from the overwhelmed water-treatment system. This caused Grand Haven to close its beaches until the coliform bacteria counts decreased to safe levels again. Grand Rapids has taken steps to correct this situation and upgrade its water-treatment plants.

But how, I wonder, could this have been allowed to continue for so many years? And Grand Rapids is only one of the many cities that dump sewage into the lake after heavy rains.

This is a minor example of the harm that has been and continues to be done to the lake. There are areas along the lake and its rivers that have been dumping grounds for industry in the past and have been cleaned up. Some of the removed sediment and soil have been too toxic to treat or dump elsewhere, so it has been entombed in concrete vaults along the lakeshore, like the one in Montague.

Egypt has their ancient pyramids, where kings and their riches were transported to the gods. Modern America has its toxic tombs, where man-made chemicals never before seen on earth are kept sequestered from nature so they will bring no further harm.

There are many parts of the lake where you can probably drink unfiltered water safely, especially if you go offshore a bit. All of the Great Lakes, I've read, are considered to be potable – if you dip a cup in the middle of the lake. The sheer volume of water makes one want to think that any impurities will be diluted near to the point of zero. But, consider this: the retention time for Lake Michigan – that is, the average time the water or any contaminate spends there – is 99 years. What we dump into the lake will mostly be with us for a lifetime.

Many compounds accumulate in the creatures living in the lake. Polychlorinated Biphenyls (PCBs) are the prime example of this; the pollutant is found in riverbeds and along the shallows of the lake where it was freely dumped before being regulated.

This compound is fat-soluble, so it does not dissolve in the water, so it should be safe to dump it, right? Well, not when you consider that it can enter the food chain. The fish at the top of the food chain retain all of the chemicals they eat in smaller fish, and the compounds accumulate in their fatty tissue. The larger the fish, the more toxic – ounce for ounce – its flesh.

When will this change? When will regulations be strengthened to decrease pollution and the introduction of additional invasive species? How are the lakes to continue to be a priority if people – especially kids – didn't care about them? I thought back to the Inland Seas Education Center and how important their work is to achieve lasting conservation of the lake.

The most invasive species of all

I began to formulate the idea that the most invasive species of all is probably man. I saw the harm that man had done to the lake, and was appalled. I should probably qualify the "man" as immigrants and their descendants, not Native Americans. The native tribes, for the most part, seemed to have a culture of honoring the land, lakes, and animals. To take only what is needed to survive, and to live in harmony with their environment.

In contrast, the early immigrants to America were, necessarily, bold, risk-taking people. They were out to establish themselves in this new land. They took all they could from the land, from the lake, from the forests, and didn't think much about the future of the environment. It must have seemed a land without end to them, but we know better. We have proven many times that we can make things "end."

The phrase that comes to mind is that some animals encountered by the pioneers were "hunted to near extinction."

The culture of the Native Americans who lived in balance with the natural world is one the rest of us would do well to study and adopt. Even today, there are tribes who are supporting green technology because it is good for the planet, like the Aleut people in Alaska harnessing the wind, or the Ute tribe in Colorado investing in a company that grows algae to convert to biodiesel. These tribes seem to be taking a longer view with their investments. The question is not "How much will we make next quarter?" but "How will this benefit my grandchildren?"

Will our actions pass the "seventh generation" test? I think of sewage and chemical pollutants dumped into the lake, and believe we can and must do better.

To the Straits

After Harbor Springs, I had a 51-mile crescent of lakeshore to walk across the northwest shores on Michigan's Lower Peninsula, a path that would take me to the Mackinac Bridge. This three-day hike covered some remote areas, including Wilderness State Park, which sets aside over 8,000 acres on the point of land (plus two large islands) west of Mackinaw City.

I hardly met a soul along the shore for most of this stretch. The shoreline varied underfoot from small, rounded rocks, to sand, to larger baseball-to-football sized rocks.

Often, there were laundry-basket-sized boulders sitting in the shallow water in a mélange of beautiful colors and patterns. Solid black rocks sat next to granite boulders of swirled orange and black and cream. A few steps further, there would be a solid peach boulder next to one of swirled peach and gray and cream, then a tan rock striped with black.

On a beach south of Cross Village, I came across the largest mound of zebra mussel shells I had ever seen. It had been deposited parallel to the waterline and into a yard-high and 5-foot wide windrow that stretched for over 50 feet. There must have been some remarkable confluence of waves and currents to bring the shells to this place, and then a perfect wave action to mound them up so neatly. They were bleached almost completely free of their black stripes and reflected the sun like a fresh snowbank.

I walked to the middle and carefully sat down. The shells shifted a bit, then settled into a comfortable seat. Scooping up two handfuls of shells from either side of me, I brought my hands together and studied the hundreds of shells. As I moved my fingers, the shells made a gentle, wind-chime, tinkling sound. I allowed them to pour through my fingers to join the mound of shells at my feet.

It was a ways north of Cross Village that I encountered a little chirping shore bird that kept darting ahead of me as I walked. It was my first piping plover *(Charadrius melodus)* along this stretch. This is a protected bird, endangered due to loss of habitat. I stopped for a minute, not wanting to scare it. It stopped running and seemed to wait for me to continue. I stayed close to the water, not wanting to disturb its nesting area. It nests on the ground, so its eggs and chicks are vulnerable to predation by dogs and other animals.

The bird does sprinting spurts in front of me for probably a half mile, then it finally takes off, flying low over the water and circling back to where he and I first met. I watch his flight, then continue walking and see two young women approaching. As the gap closes between us, I see that one carries a big telescope on a tripod and some serious binoculars are around her neck. The other woman holds a clipboard.

"Hi," I say as we get within conversing distance. "Are you studying the piping plovers?"

"Yes," the one with the clipboard says. "This is our second year collecting data."

"Dream job. Out on the lake and all." I look up at the brilliant blue sky. "Especially on a day like this."

The other woman lifts the binoculars, then sets up the scope on the tripod. "Are you hiking to Wilderness Park?" she asks before looking through the scope.

"All the way around the lake this year. I started in Chicago."

They both stare at me. "Cool."

They continue to scan the area with their devices. "That was 'Eyebrow,'" the woman says looking back in the scope. She meant the plover I had just encountered.

"We give them nicknames," the clipboard woman says, making a note.

"How are the birds doing?"

"Their numbers are holding steady."

"Is it okay to walk like I did, by the waterline? I kept giving him a chance to fly and loop around."

"Staying by the water is great. There's a nesting area not too far from here. It's roped off, but you can pass between it and the water," the one with the clipboard says.

"He's posturing," says scope woman.

"What does that mean?" I ask.

Clipboard woman says, "He's trying to get a mate. They really don't get all that aggressive."

"Hence the scope to see if they raise their eyebrows?" I laugh.

"Yeah," scope woman laughs. "Hey, you'll walk the Upper Peninsula, right?"

"Next month."

"Near the town of Gulliver, you'll see a great stretch of beach. The plovers nest there, too."

"Great. I'll look for them. So, do you think their numbers will increase?"

Clipboard woman smiles and says, "We saw the first babies in the park yesterday. Every new chick helps."

I wish them well, and the little birds, too, and press on north, up the beach. About two miles further I see my first piping plover chicks – tiny puffballs of mostly white feathers on orange, stick legs – darting after their parents on the sand.

You've been out here a *looong* time

Wilderness Park is aptly named. I saw butterflies flocking (yes, actually flying around in groups), geese a-laying, blue herons and sandhill cranes a-stalking, frogs a-croaking, plover chicks a-piping. I also saw the sun-bleached bones of many a wild meal and large, lazy fish swimming in the shallows. I even saw a far-off streak of tawny-colored animal chasing something low in the grass. There had been sightings of cougar in the park, but I could not confirm if this was one of the big cats or not.

I just hoped it caught whatever it was chasing – and had a filling lunch.

As I neared the tip of land that juts out into the lake to form the most westerly part of the park, I planned on going inland at a boat ramp. These are always reliable routes to get from the lake back to civilization. About a mile before I reached it, I came upon a wetland. Inland, however, instead of the land becoming more firm and dry, it turned into a bog with some very deep, murky, mucky holes. I backtracked and cut inland even further into the dense woods skirting the bog and found myself in a place I suspect no human had traversed for decades.

It was a primordial forest so dense that little sunlight reached the ground. The floor of the forest was covered in a thick, mossy mat that cushioned every step. The smell was loamy and alive.

I was enchanted – until I tried moving through it. There were downed trees everywhere. The dead, lower branches of trees often formed a thicket that I had to crash through. I finally reached a small stream and took the time to zip the legs of my pants back on to protect me from the swarming mosquitoes and probable ticks. I should have jumped into the shallow, winding stream and followed it inland, but my GPS showed a trail not too far away. The problem with moving through the dense forest was that after I had crashed and ducked, scurried under and climbed over obstacles for twenty feet or so, I'd check my GPS to find that I had veered wildly off course during my struggles. I'd make a correction and thrash another twenty feet, then have to correct again.

When I eventually broke out of the branches onto the narrow trail, I was elated and relieved. Had I not had the GPS, I'd probably still be out there, crashing around in a giant circle.

About an eighth of a mile along the trail, I crossed over that little stream that I should have followed. Lesson learned.

I followed the trail and then a dirt road to the north side of the park. There were some men loading kayaks onto a van near the water. One of them looked me over from head to boots and said, "You've been out here a *looong* time!" Not sure just how battered I looked, I nodded, smoothed down my hair in back (dislodging several twigs still entangled there) and answered, "Yep."

I looked down saw that my pants were covered with spiderwebs that I had been walking through for miles. Even though I hadn't seen most of them in the darkness of the woods, they still clung to me, their ghostly webbing studded with an occasional wrapped-up insect lunch that came along for the ride. It appeared as though I had emerged from a cocoon, a woman just metamorphosed.

When I reached the edge of the lake on the north side of the park, I looked out at an enormous lake freighter. I turned to my right and got my first glimpse of the Mackinac Bridge.

It was much closer than I expected, and it was a shock to see it so clearly. Since I began the trek in Chicago, the bridge represented the farthest point from my start (and finish) line. And on the distant shores, I saw Michigan's wild Upper Peninsula stretching out before me, across the Straits of Mackinac.

Half-way

On the final day of this segment, I reached the 500-mile mark of the Lake Trek. I was in a residential area within the city limits of Mackinaw City, and there was a vacant lakeshore lot for sale. I walked out on the lot and looked at the lake. I had conquered half of the distance around this body of water, and I took a moment to feel that accomplishment in my bones and breath and body. I thought back to the beginning, that cool morning in March on Chicago's Navy Pier jutting out into this very body of water.

I wondered if the currents had brought any of those same droplets of water that lapped at Navy Pier that day all the way up to the Straits of Mackinac. Were they passing by even at that moment as I looked out over the water? Had they followed me all this way?

I looked east and studied the bridge connecting Michigan's two peninsulas. Then, I looked at the expansive straits – that mass of deep, fast-moving water that connects Lakes Michigan and Huron. Five miles across the water, the shoreline of the Upper Peninsula of Michigan stretched until it disappeared at the horizon.

This had been the longest segment I had walked so far at 9 days, and the most physically demanding. Exhaustion and elation blended together as I considered that magic number: I had walked 500 miles. I had walked the smoky, sooty southern edge of the lake, through the wide beaches of the Indiana Dunes National Lakeshore, then crossed into Michigan and followed its sandy western edge to the tip of the peninsula, the straits, the bridge.

All this time, the lake had held my left hand. If the waves reached for me, I leapt to my right. Then I'd return to walking, whenever I could, just at the height of the waves' reach. There was a communication between stride and slosh of water, of step and crest, of muscle and pull and push of the winds. A harmony had been established between the lake that had been alive for thousands of years and me, a being of less than fifty years, half-a-sigh in time's eye.

As I completed the final miles into Mackinaw City, I realized that the most remote and rugged portion of the trek still stretched before me. To give some perspective on Michigan's Upper Peninsula, it makes up a third of the landmass of the state, but contains only about 3% of its population. There is a lot of open land there – expansive wetlands, mountains in the western part, and plenty of moose, bear, and wolves.

My plan was to take ten days to span the southern edge of the Upper Peninsula. Then I'd continue on the following segment – down the west side of Green Bay and then across Wisconsin's Door Peninsula – after a two-day rest in the city of Escanaba. That meant I'd be hiking for 19 days total.

Even though I felt stronger at this point, and more assured in my skills to move through the land, I still wondered what wild adventures awaited in Michigan's untamed Upper Peninsula.

Between Segments 6 and 7

June 17–July 2

The Ocean

Two days after getting back from Mackinaw City, I packed up and flew with my sons down to my sister's place in North Carolina for a mini-family reunion. My sister-in-law, Mary Jo, drove up from Atlanta with her two kids and my mom and brother Phil and sister Leslie also gathered there. It was a time of boogie-boarding and seafood-eating and sunscreen-slathering.

I enjoy the ocean. There's something about seeing a crab dart sideways in the shallows, or to digging up a handful of sand crabs, or watching a pair of dolphin swim parallel to shore that makes it feel full of salty life. As much as I enjoyed my time on the Carolina beaches, though, I still felt the pull of fresh water, the call of the Lake Trek while I splashed in the Atlantic.

My favorite part of Leslie's place is her front porch. It runs the length of the house, and is fully screened. Les has furnished the ample space with Adirondack chairs and a daybed with lots of pillows. We gather there after the sun sets and listen to the Carolina night sounds.

"You seem a little distant," Les says. "What'cha thinking about?"

I'm slouching on one end of the day bed, surrounded by pillows. She sits on the other end. I curl into a ball and pull a pillow under my head. "The Upper Peninsula."

Leslie waits, then prods me, "And?"

"I guess I'm a little overwhelmed."

"You? Overwhelmed?" she laughs. "Finally?"

"Yeah, finally. Just a little, though." We laugh ourselves silly.

"Well, I felt completely overwhelmed after three hours walking the trek with you. You'll be fine. Take it a day at a time." She pats my leg, then pokes my calf muscle, then my thigh with her finger. "Jeez, your legs are like iron! Stop whining!"

She goes inside the house. When she comes back out, she is carrying two margaritas with salt.

The Island

Three days after returning home to Battle Creek, I pack up again and head north with my sons and Phil to Mackinac Island. We planned to spend a few days together before I continued the Lake Trek through the wilds of the Upper Peninsula (the UP, as Michiganders call it).

Mackinac Island is a relaxing place. There are no cars allowed, so the sounds are gentle. Horses and bikes and feet are the only ways to get around the island, and people generally slow down and breathe a bit easier there. It was good to be on the island with my boys.

I had planned to spend most of July on the Lake Trek for several reasons. My sons would be on their own adventures this month: Lucas to three weeks of piano camp, and Ben to Germany to take two classes. I coordinated the next two segments as a continuous walk during this time, because returning home between the segments would be difficult. Segment 7 ended and 8 began in the city of Escanaba, near the western end of the UP, the furthest break point from my home.

Our time on Mackinac Island goes by at a leisurely pace. We walk, bike around the island, and eat lots of fudge and ice cream. We find a putt-putt course on one end of the main street right along the water. Usually I hate miniature golf with its windmills and clown heads (I have an aversion to clowns), but the course on the island is a series of nicely manicured greens without all the scary statuary.

I pay for the four of us, and we choose putters and brightly colored golf balls. Phil grabs the official scorecard and a stubby pencil. We head to the first hole.

Lucas is quite serious as he lines up each shot. Ben, on the other hand, is Zen about life and is out to have some fun. Often, he lines up a shot, closes his eyes, and putts. This infuriates Lucas who takes several practice strokes before putting. Phil – the least athletic of all of us, he has never in his life played a round of true golf – makes several awesome putts.

After the ninth hole, sure enough, it is Uncle Phil who is in the lead.

Lucas looks at him and says, "How do you *do* that?"

Phil looks off over the expansive water and says, "Skill."

Lucas buckles down even more on the second half of the course, scoping out the curves and rises of the greens from several angles before putting. At the last hole, Luc is two strokes back, Ben and I are three strokes back, and Phil – against all odds – is still firmly in the lead.

"You go first, Uncle Phil. I'll go last," Luc says.

Ben drops his ball on the green, lines it up, then looks back at Lucas while he putts. His ball goes off the rim of the cup and stops about a foot away.

"Oh, come *on!*" Luc says.

Phil and I putt several feet from the hole, then Lucas places his ball on the green. He studies the slope from several angles.

"Just hit the ball!" Ben says.

Luc lines up his shot, and putts. He gets a hole-in-one. "Yes!" he shouts. Ben finishes in one more stroke, and I take two. So it's down to Phil and Luc.

"Okay, Uncle Phil. If you get it in three, we're tied," Luc says.

"Why would I take three when I only need two?" Phil deadpans. Then Phil nonchalantly sinks his second shot, a tricky four-foot putt.

Lucas demands a rematch the next day, and we return to the course. Phil somehow wins again.

"How did you *do* that?" Lucas asks as we walk our putters back to the kiosk.

"I came out to the course last night while you were sleeping to practice," Phil deadpans.

"You *what?!*" Lucas says. It takes a moment for him to realize that his Uncle Phil is pulling his leg.

I embraced my sons on the morning of our last day together. The boys and Phil were heading back to Mackinaw City. Ben and Luc would drive home from there, and Phil would pick up my car and cross the bridge to shadow me through Segment 7. I had decided against camping on Segment 7, but planned to camp here and there on Segment 8.

It was strange to separate from them like this after three days of being so close together, and I will admit to getting a little misty as my ferry pulled away from the dock. Once out of the harbor, my ferry accelerated and a rooster tail of white water shot up behind the boat. I gave a final wave, then turned my eyes forward, across the water to Michigan's wild Upper Peninsula.

Some people get stronger and stronger as they exercise. I tend to strengthen for a while, but then reach a point where I need a break in order to recuperate. I needed this time between Segments 6 and 7 to rest and gather myself for the challenges that stretched out before me, the next 500 miles.

Segment 7

July 2–11
St. Ignace to Escanaba
161 miles in 10 days

Total Trek Mileage: 663 miles

The joining of the lakes

Lakes Michigan and Huron have a connection that is unique among the Great Lakes. All other connections are rivers: the St. Marys River drains Superior into Huron, the Detroit River links Huron and Erie, and Erie drains into Ontario via the Niagara River. Lakes Michigan and Huron, however, are joined at the Straits of Mackinac where they meld at their northern ends.

The watery connection is five miles wide at its narrowest point where the bridge spans. Its depths reach over 300 feet in places gouged out by the glaciers.

Mackinac Island is, technically, in Lake Huron, and the boat that ferried me from the island to the Upper Peninsula docked in the city of St. Ignace on the Lake Huron side. The stroll through the small town of St. Ignace was a gentle beginning to Segment 7, which promised to be a remote and wild westerly hike of over 150 miles from St. Ignace to the city of Escanaba. I walked for several miles before seeing the bridge again and feeling back at home as I returned to the shores of Lake Michigan.

I saw many signs advertising pasties as I walked through town, and I stopped at a roadside place that sold them. This meat and vegetable pie, about as big as a large hand, was an important meal for the iron miners in the UP. They could take the sturdy pie down into the mine, then warm it with their torches. It is a hearty meal, packed with potatoes and meat and rutabaga. I could only eat half of it, then stored the rest in my pack.

Once out of the city, I made my way closer to the lake. Wildflowers carpeted the shoulders of the side roads and bobbed their happy faces at me. Orange lilies dotted patches of yellow daisies, and I saw my first lady-slipper of the Lake Trek there. This is a rather rare and beautiful temperate orchid. It has a large, rounded, light-pink lower part of the flower – the slipper – topped with several pointed, white leaves like silk laces. I hadn't seen one in years, but several clustered together along the roadside there, thriving and exotic.

I followed the banks of a small river down to the lake and began walking along the weedy, mucky shoreline. Soon I was in a wetland and had to cut back inland to the closest road. I was almost 15 miles out of St. Ignace when the shoreline finally opened up into an expansive, sandy beach that stretched for miles. Plants grew on the foredunes all the way down to near the waterline. Grasses and flowers covered the sand, stabilizing the dune formations. Fat bumblebees worked the light-pink flowers of the endangered pitcher's thistle plants, and ladybugs polka-dotted the grasses and ferns.

I came across several areas on this beach that had been cordoned off for the piping plovers. These areas – unlike the ones I had seen in the Lower Peninsula – were roped off down into the water. I cut inland, crossing house-sized dunes, to respect these nesting areas and wished the little, chirping birds well in their nesting efforts.

Highway 2 skirted the beach for many miles and at one point got close enough to the lake that chunks of white limestone had been placed on the narrow beach to keep the waves from washing away the road bed. Scrambling over the rocks was fun for a while, but then I noticed the multitude of fat, quarter-sized spiders spanning every available gap between the stones. I normally don't mind spiders, but these guys seemed to follow my every movement like they were wondering how best to coordinate as a pack and wrap me up for dinner. Since Highway 2 was so close, I jumped up onto the shoulder of the road and walked it into the town of Brevort.

The million-dollar bridge over the ten-cent river

The Cut River Bridge spans 600 feet across a narrow ravine. The top of the bridge is almost 150 feet above the Cut River, which really isn't a river at all, but a shallow, narrow stream. It is one of the most photographed bridges in Michigan.

When I was hiking through, cars were detoured around it because it was under construction. I walked past the detour signs. It was eerie to be on the road with no traffic and no sounds other than what the wind and birds made. I had hoped to talk to the construction workers to see if I could still cross the bridge on foot, but as I got nearer, I realized that the site was completely deserted. It was the Friday of the 4th of July weekend. All the workers were on holiday.

I passed all the barricades and cranes. Then I passed a row of metal cages full of two-foot-long bolts, nuts and square, steel plates. There was a makeshift table of planks on saw horses, set for someone to assemble the bolts and plates and nuts into a small reinforcing piece for the massive bridge. As I approached the edge, I noticed the concrete road surface had been removed, exposing the bridge's I-beam skeleton. I could look through the beams to the creek far below. Boards were placed along the edges for workers to walk. It looked precarious to me, and I had no desire to try to balance my way across the torn-up bridge, so I walked the 231 wooden steps to the bottom of the gorge, hiked underneath, and up the other side. There are massive, arched, stone support columns down in the gorge, and the steel – painted a deep, forest green – gracefully swoops from one arch to the next to span the depression. It's a lovely bridge, and it was a treat to have it all to myself, to be able to listen to the birds calling, to the rustling of deer in the woods and the murmuring lake instead of cars and trucks passing overhead.

Hiking west from Epoufette Bay, I had a day mostly on the lake. The shoreline varied from powdered sand to scattered boulders to wetlands dotted with blue irises to forest, then back to sand. There were deep streams that I had to wade with my boots looped over my neck and my pack balanced on my head. It was a nice way to cool down, and I stirred up some fat brown trout as I tiptoed across the silty stream bed. I sat on the high bank after crossing to let my pants dry off a bit.

It is strange to be in a place where you feel you could sit for days or even weeks and months and never see another person. There were no trails, no human footsteps had fallen here for many long years. A thicket protected the far bank of the stream, preventing larger animals from wandering here.

They would take an easier way. I looked at all the little scratches on my arms. Yes, animals would be smarter and would take another route. I heard no human noise other than my own breath, and only my modern clothing and gear and a lone jet contrail told me I was living in modern times.

Further along the shoreline, I passed a small island that was a rookery for gulls. They gave up quite a racket when I passed. The lakeshore was strewn with gull guano and feathers and, occasionally, a dead chick that had washed ashore. Very close to the nesting island was a campground. The people staying there had the road on one side and hundreds of rowdy gulls on the other and a bird-befouled beach.

East of the city of Nabinway, I encountered the point furthest north on Lake Michigan. Since I had already hiked the southern curve of the lake, this meant that I had walked its entire length south to north. In 1805 when Congress created the Territory of Michigan, it used this geographic point as the western edge of the territory. Beyond this line was Indian Territory until 1818 when Michigan was temporarily expanded to stretch all the way to the Mississippi River.

I stood at the apex of the lake and looked south. It was over three hundred miles across the water to the southern rim of the lake. Only five days into the trek, I had stood at its southernmost point looking north.

Now I looked back on my former self, standing cold and sore on that far shore. Those intervening months and miles had shaped me; I was stronger. I could read the lake now, the shoreline, the vegetation. A synchrony had been established between my footfall and the rhythm of the waves. I felt more connected to this vast body of water than ever before.

The first four nights of this segment, Phil and I stayed at a scenic hotel on the outskirts of St. Ignace. Each day when he picked me up, we retraced the route that I had already walked. Day after day, the evening ride lengthened. I had been averaging 15 miles per day on the trek to this point, so after three days we had quite a ride – especially with the Cut River Bridge detour – to return to our hotel. Another thing we kept returning to was the Mackinac Bridge, as our hotel room overlooked the straits. Each night I was able to look out on the gorgeous bridge and watch the moon lift itself into the night sky above it.

On our last night there, July 4th, Phil and I were treated to Mackinaw

City's fireworks exploding above the Mighty Mac Bridge. They illuminated the sky with red and green and bright white while the graceful bridge draped with its necklace of lights held its place in the gap where the two Great Lakes merged.

Summer a long time comin'

Anytime I walked the shoreline where there were private homes, I wondered if people minded me crossing their property, if they would be angry with me if they saw me strolling across their "private" land. I was even more concerned in the remote areas where few people probably ever wandered.

After a little research in planning the trip, I was prepared to gently defend my legal right (at least in Michigan) to walk on the shoreline that had been "scrubbed free of vegetation" as determined by Michigan's Supreme Court.

Whenever I saw people, I always waved at them, sitting out on their deck or in their yards. No one had shown any hostility to me on my trek to this point. I noticed a difference in the UP: they were even friendlier. In the earlier part of the trek when I would wave to someone, they'd often study me for a moment, then raise a hand in tentative reply. In the UP, though, they immediately waved back, and not just with their hand, but with a huge arm-sweeping movement over their head. Sometimes, I'd see several people hanging out on their deck; I'd give a wave, and watch everyone leap to their feet to wave back at me.

When I got the chance to speak with yoopers (as they affectionately call themselves), they often used the sentence, "Summer was a long time comin' this year." It was true for all of Michigan, but even more so for the UP. I think they were glad to see me, no matter where I was walking. I probably could have walked into their house, grabbed a cold drink from their fridge, then joined these friendly people for a chat on their deck.

Since summer was late, the lake was cooler than normal for this time of year. July 5 was the first really hot day I had in the UP, and the morning warmed up so fast that a dense fog formed over the still cold lake. I had gotten pretty adept at picking my way along the shoreline through rocks and bogs and wetlands, but I needed to see the vegetation to do this. This day, though, the shoreline was shrouded in fog so thick that I couldn't see even five feet in front of me. I had walked in fog before, but along a wide, sandy beach. It was a little creepy, but it was safe. This stretch west of Nabinway and down the lee side of the bay, however, would certainly contain some serious wetlands.

I had learned that when a shoreline had open water and was on the windward side of the lake, I could expect a relatively sandy shoreline. Most of the west side of Michigan's Lower Peninsula was like this. The wind and wave action had piled sand along the way, and then lofted it up into dunes in many places. As the land undulated into bays and inlets, it is protected from these forces, and the shore is often rocky, swampy, and marshy. The southern edge of the UP has two smaller peninsulas that reach out into the lake, the Garden and the Stonington. They are close together, too, so they shield each other from wave action. I expected wetlands there.

West of Nabinway, I made the difficult decision to stay on the road all day instead of getting lost in a bog in the fog. It turned my 15-mile day into 19, and I rarely had even a glimpse of the lake. I got to watch the wind play with a field of green hay, and I sucked the nectar from many fat clover blooms to see what bee's life was like.

And I had a conversation with a bird. It was a little songbird, probably a white-throated sparrow. Using the do-re-mi scale, the bird sang a clear *mi-do* descending song, and I whistled it back to him: *mi-do.* He answered again, *mi-do.* I began adding to the song. *Mi-do-do* was answered with *mi-do-do.* And I changed it up: *mi-do-do-do-mi.* Amazingly, he riffed on that by answering, *mi-do-do-do-mi-do.*

We chatted like this while I walked the road; the bird flitted along in the shrubs and trees, singing his little heart out. At one point, we were singing over ten notes at a stretch to each other. I never did get a good look at him, but I hoped he wasn't too heartbroken that I kept walking as I whistled.

I had been hiking south for hours and had almost reached the lake again. The day was hot and the road was also radiating heat, so I was soaked with sweat. Three species of flies – a horse fly, a deer fly, and a regular housefly – had been buzzing a wide circle around me for miles. I tried many different approaches to whacking them with my hat and was amazed at their ability to evade my attacks. In frustration I used my stick, too, spinning and thrashing with it.

There are times one is glad to be in a remote area, and as I stepped outside my manic, fly-fighting self for a moment, I got a picture of what I must have looked like. The rare times I heard a vehicle, I'd stop fighting the flies while the car or truck rolled past. This allowed the flies to buzz closer, to tighten the noose, as it were. Yes, it was a war, and I was determined to not let them bite me, especially the deer fly. I know, you'd think I'd want to avoid the larger horse fly, but I am allergic to deer flies and swell up to mutant proportions if bitten.

Finally, Phil caught up with me and pulled over. I tossed my walking stick into the trunk and jumped in the front seat. Phil's eyes got wide as he sniffed the air I brought with me.

"What?" I said. "That's the smell of the great outdoors!"

Phil pulled back onto the road and accelerated.

"It might be outdoors," he quipped, "but it certainly isn't 'great.'"

The "only choice"

West of my stopping point that day was a large limestone quarry. These areas are always gated and restricted, and because this one was bordered by wetlands to the north, I was worried that I might not be able to get around it. I began the next day across the harbor from the quarry at the Seul Choix Point and the lighthouse there.

While Little Sable is my favorite Lake Michigan lighthouse, Seul Choix is probably a close second. While Little Sable is a brown brick tower standing alone on the vast lakeshore, Seul Choix (French for "only choice") is on a wooded and rocky hook of land that reaches out into the lake to form a safe bay. The lighthouse is brick, painted white with accents of green on the curved brackets that support the upper catwalk. Topping the light chamber is a rounded, red metal roof.

From this point, I walked most of the way into the city of Manistique in one day. The two piping plover researchers that I had met in Wilderness State Park told me to look for a sandy beach east of Manistique near the town of Gulliver, so I was eager to hike this day back on sand. As I made my way along the shoreline from the lighthouse, a massive, sloped limestone shelf extended from the vegetation line out into the lake. At one point, there was a rock island offshore, and a bald eagle sat there watching the water. I had seen several of these distinctive birds fly over while I hiked – once with a large fish in its talons – but I had not seen one so close and still.

I later heard that when they had celebrated the restoration of the Seul Choix Lighthouse, a bald eagle had flown over the gathering. This was considered to be good luck. This eagle looked pretty comfortable on his island a couple of miles from the lighthouse, and I wondered if it was he who had bestowed the fly-over blessing.

The going was rugged for several miles, since limestone in many shapes studded the shoreline. Sometimes it was a scattering of square boulders, at times like row after row of jagged teeth in the jaw of the shore. Often there were flat, stone expanses with wide fractures that I had to leap. Then, the stone would rise up in walls taller than me and I would have to climb up and over them, once walking along the wide top as the wall hugged the shoreline.

Often, there would be a small hole in the rock face where sand or soil had gathered, then a seed happened upon, to now bloom in the gray rock expanse. It was shocking to see a burst of yellow or blue flowers in the middle of all that stone. Once, I saw a puddle in a stony depression filled with resting tadpoles that wriggled to life when I moved my stick gently through the top of the water.

Soon, the limestone shelf gave way to intermittent stretches of sand, then, all at once, opened up to miles of wide, sandy beach. I was so delighted to be back on sand that I took off my boots and walked in the water, barefoot, for miles. It was along this stretch that I saw a few scattered people, including one large group. This family had three generations gathered on the lake, and the two smallest kids, a boy and a girl, were digging in the sand near the water.

The girl, probably 6 or 7, ran up to me and shouted, "What are you doing?"

I waved my walking stick at the expanse of water and said, "I'm walking all the way around this lake!"

She laughed and said, "You'd better hurry up! You're going to be SIXTY when you're done!"

Most people – previously, me included – cannot fathom walking 1,000 miles. When I started clipping off 15 miles a day, I could feel the miles stacking up beneath my boots. By the time my path met up with this little girl, I had walked over 570 miles, so I knew it was not an impossible undertaking. And, though I would celebrate one birthday during the trek, I would certainly not be 60 when I finished.

The shoreline along the city of Manistique has a three-mile boardwalk and paved path meandering along the lake and through the various types of shore habitats. There are areas with limestone, sand, interdunal wetlands, swales, and wet flats. All are unique and attract various animals and insects and birds along the shore.

Manistique was a big lumbering town – like most coastal river towns in Michigan – during the mid to late 1800s. It is estimated that over 5 million tons of sawdust were produced in Manistique during the lumbering years. Much of it was towed out into the lake and dumped. One would think that over the last 100 years the sawdust and stray rough-sawn lumber would have deteriorated and disappeared, but this is not the case. There are stretches of shoreline where I walked on a foot or two or three of ancient, shredded wood. Offshore, I could see deposits of wood chips and sawdust blackened with age on the bottom of the lake. Along many stretches, there were rough-sawn planks ranging from three to ten feet long – and, occasionally, a massive, square-cut beam – washed up on the beach.

So common were these planks that kids had often stood them up on end in a circle like a wooden teepee. I had walked by many old lumbering towns without seeing this scattered legacy. The cooler water at the north end of the lake may have something to do with the preservation of these reminders of Michigan's logging days.

I followed the curve of the shoreline partway down the east side of the Garden Peninsula, then began the next day on the west side, at Fayette Historic State Park and hiked north.

Fayette Historic State Park

While in the wilds of the UP, I didn't expect to find a connection to the heavy industrial southern rim of the lake, but it's there. There are large deposits of iron ore in the UP in three Iron Ranges of mountains: the Gogebic, Marquette, and Menominee. Before the city of Fayette was founded, raw iron ore was transported by ship from the mines in the UP and upper Minnesota to the refineries at the south end of the lake. This ore was refined to remove the oxygen and silica to produce usable iron. The iron companies of the day were spending a lot of money transporting the impurities (up to 40 percent of the weight of the ore).

They came up with this idea: instead of transporting 10 tons of ore south where it would be refined to 6 tons of iron, why not refine the ore near the mines, then transport only the refined product south?

Shortly after the Civil War, the Jackson Iron Company sent a fellow named Fayette Brown into the UP to find a location for a refinery. The site had to have several things: a large deposit of limestone, large stands of hardwoods, and a deep harbor. The town of Fayette was named after the man, and it exploded to a population of almost 500 people dedicated to working in this iron-smelting operation.

To put this into historical perspective, it was founded two years after the Civil War. This was a war where men were still taking the time to ram a metal ball and charge down the barrel of their musket. This was an era of using charcoal to smelt ore. While we now think of charcoal as briquettes in a bag, at that time it was made by roasting hardwood in a kiln. Think about what's left in your fireplace after the fire dies. That's wood charcoal, and they were able to produce it in large quantities by loading tall, brick kilns with several cords of wood, and then roasting it over many hours.

Large swaths of forest were felled to feed these kilns, and the charcoal in turn fed the blast furnaces. It took about an acre of woods to smelt two tons of iron. Limestone, a very hard form called dolomite, was added to the melting ore. The calcium in the limestone binds to the silicate impurities in the ore. The byproduct of this reaction, called slag, floats to the top of the molten ore. The purified iron can then be drained out of the bottom of the furnace and cooled into bars in depressions in the sand. These bars are called pig iron because of the way they line up in the sand along a central trough.

The town of Fayette had shops, hotels and restaurants, and workers' cabins clustered near the shoreline. The town thrived from 1867 to 1891. During this time, Fayette produced a quarter million tons of pig iron, and most of the Garden Peninsula was denuded of hardwood in the process.

Now, the place has been restored as a historic town site and state park. For over a century, waves have tumbled the slag that was dumped into the lake. The once-jagged shards are now smooth, rounded rocks in colors ranging from turquoise to purples to swirled, milky blues. The shoreline there is piled with these bluish rocks, making it look like they are reflecting the very colors of the vast sky.

Many of the buildings and furnaces still stand, or have been recreated.

The hills are covered with second-growth forests, and the soaring limestone cliffs still encircle the deep, clear-water harbor. The limestone cliffs along the lake here provide a unique habitat for several species of land snails.

This is one of my favorite spots in the UP because of its natural beauty and sense of walking back in time as you explore the park. A piece of history has been preserved. While most of Michigan's lakeshore parks preserve a slice of wilderness, this park preserves a slice of 19th-century life along with evidence and artifacts of the Chippewa tribes that inhabited the area long before iron ore was ever extracted from the heart of the mountains.

The Garden Peninsula reaches toward the Door Peninsula, helping to form Green Bay to the west. If you look at a map of the Great Lakes and follow the curve of these two peninsulas along the southern edge of the UP, down the Bruce Peninsula in Lake Huron and then to Niagara Falls, you've traced the Niagara Escarpment. This cap of hard limestone along this arc is the reason that the three peninsulas and Niagara Falls are there, instead of having been scraped away by the mile-high glaciers that gouged out the lakes so long ago.

All along the Garden Peninsula, there are outcroppings of this limestone cap. Sometimes it is in the form of a soaring white rock cliff that falls off into the water, sometimes a white, 8-foot wall running along the road, sometimes in a pile of broken limestone gathered and stacked from a farmer's field.

There is, as one might expect given its name, a lot of farming along the Garden Peninsula. After the refinery at Fayette closed, many of the workers stayed to farm the deforested peninsula. I passed one place that had a "Centennial Farm" designation from the Michigan Historical Commission. This farm has been worked by the same family for over one hundred years.

I walked along the water where I could, but mostly had to keep to the main road because with each undulation of the shore, a wetland or swamp had formed. These areas are great for boaters and ducks and fish, but not so much for a hiker.

Near the town of Garden, there was a platform erected on which an osprey had assembled a huge nest of sticks. I had seen many of these great fishing birds near the ocean, but this was the first I had seen around the Great Lakes. As I approached, the bird took flight and continued to circle high above me until I was well past its nest.

On the shoulder of the road, I found a dead but perfectly intact dragonfly. I gently gathered it up, and its claw-like feet latched onto my finger. At home, I had occasionally disentangled one of these beautiful insects from the netting placed around my garden in an effort to keep the deer from feasting there. The tired insects rarely lingered in my hand once free and would launch back onto the breeze where they lived.

This one, in death, had time to spare. It had not died from trauma since even its delicate and transparent wings were unbroken, still attached at the perfect angle to take flight. I studied its bulging, blue eyes and wondered how it flew through a world seen through so many lenses. I stroked the hunchback of its thorax, the home to the power for those broad wings, and noticed the tribal stripes there and down to the end of the abdomen. Such attention was given to its every detail. I nestled it on a plant and continued walking.

Toward the end of this day's hike, I could look across Big Bay De Noc and see the Stonington Peninsula. In between was an arc of land that I walked in one day.

Monarchs, piping plovers and black Labs

The arc of land between the Garden and Stonington Peninsulas had one small town on it, Nahma, but was otherwise rather rugged with a few farms spliced into the woods and wetlands. The area was a haven for monarch butterflies. The roads were lined with milkweed, fallow fields given over to the milky plant.

I knew that the monarch migrated to Mexico every year, then back north to reproduce, but I had not known that the monarchs that migrate south in the fall were so many generations removed from the ones that migrated north in the spring. The monarchs which winter-over in Mexico live several months longer than usual and migrate to the southern states in the spring. There, they reproduce and die.

Their offspring, when they've changed from caterpillar to butterfly, continue the migration north, and many of them are drawn up the length of Lake Michigan to the Garden and Stonington Peninsulas in the UP. The butterflies that arrive there reproduce and die, and so do their offspring, so the migrants to Mexico in the fall are at least four generations removed from the ones that wintered-over the year before. Amazing.

The milkweed plants along the road were loaded with the fat monarch caterpillars, with their black and yellow and white stripes. Some plants were leaning from the weight of these hungry guests. The milkweed was finally in bloom, and I am continually amazed at the beauty of its flower. When thinking about the plant, most people picture the pod that hardens and pops open in the fall. From it, seeds miraculously emerge and take flight on their puff of wispy white hairs. If you happen to open a pod before it's ready, you'll see the highly organized seeds – over a 100 in a pod – perfectly arranged and overlapping with their white hairs combed neatly upward.

It is from the fertilized flowers, though, that the pods are formed. The flowers are unexpectedly beautiful. It's not a single bloom, but a cascade of up to 30 tiny flowers forming a cluster bloom. If you look closely at a single pink-and-white flower, it looks like a tiny, five-point crown. Within this crown are holes in which nectar-drinking insects might stick their legs. If they're able to extract their leg with pollen attached, then fly to another flower and again trip into a hole and deposit the pollen at the new flower, then it's pollinated. Normally, only one of the tiny flowers in each cluster will be successfully fertilized (thanks to clumsy bugs) and go on to produce a seed pod.

On this arc of land I saw wild turkey, deer, and sandhill cranes, yellow finches and sparrow hawks. There was a piping plover nesting area marked off on this stretch, with a truck parked nearby. Way out on the mucky shore, a tall man was walking and letting his two black labs frolic in the water. I like dogs, but it is a simple thing to keep them away from these clearly marked areas. He was too far out to hear me yell, so I wrote down his license plate number and called the DNR later to see if they would warn the man. The DNR said it was an *animal control* issue, not an *endangered species* issue. This seemed a little short-sighted with the fate of an endangered bird in question.

The Stonington Peninsula was part of the last stretch of the UP that I had to cover before I'd begin walking the curve of Green Bay. I began at the southernmost tip where the Point Peninsula Lighthouse stands. This structure is unusual in that it is square and rather squat instead of the typical round and slim lighthouse shape. I climbed to the top and took in the 360-degree view east to Big Bay de Noc, south to Green Bay, west to Little Bay de Noc, and north up the Stonington Peninsula. A sign near the lighthouse said that thousands of monarchs gather there to rest each fall before flying the length of Lake Michigan on their flight of more than 1,900 miles to Mexico. A flight made on whisper-thin butterfly wings.

The shoreline was rocky and weedy, and I walked it until limestone cliffs began to rise at the waterline. Across Little Bay de Noc, I could see the city of Escanaba. This was the ending point for this segment and it was a two-day hike away.

From the top of the Stonington Peninsula, it was one more day's hike to Escanaba. I crossed several large rivers. The Whitefish, Rapid and Tacoosh Rivers all feed into the very top of Little Bay de Noc. The Escanaba River joins to the south of this point. All this water supplies a variety of habitats for wildlife, and I saw many types of duck and some swans along the stretch leading to Escanaba.

Wetlands have a special serenity to them. Along this segment I had watched a swan with her signets swim in the marsh grasses, seen pairs of pintail ducks land on the water, and spied a posse of crayfish moseying sideways along the bottom of a stream. Healthy wetlands mean a healthy lake.

As I stroll through Gladstone's park near the marina, I remember that Lucas is home for this one day between his two piano camps. I pull out my phone and call home.

"Hello?" he says, his voice still sleepy.

"Luc!"

"Mom!" he says. "Where are you?"

"Still in the UP. I passed six hundred and fifty miles!"

"Wow. Cool."

"How was camp?" I ask, and we talk about his last week, what he learned, who the teachers were, how much fun he had.

"Fantastic. Are you ready for the next camp?"

"Yep. Doing my laundry right now."

"Good man! Have you heard from Ben?"

"I think we're supposed to Skype him tonight."

"Tell him I miss him and love him, okay?"

"Ah, yeah. I'll tell Dad to do that for you, okay?"

"Whatever works, Luc," we laugh together. "I'm so glad your camp went well."

"Me, too. Best ever."

"I'll let you get back to your laundry. Tell your Dad I'll call him this weekend."

"Okay. Have fun, Mom."

"You know I am."

"Yeah, crazy lake Mom," he laughs.

"Love you, Luc."

"Bye, Mom."

I walk with light steps all the way to the hotel in Escanaba, humming the songs that Lucas most loves to play on the piano.

Between Segments 7 and 8

July 12–13

Two whole days off!

Since Escanaba was so far from my home, I had decided to do Segments 7 and 8 back-to-back. I did have the foresight to schedule two days off between segments, though, to take a break in the middle of this hike of more than 300 miles. On my first day off, Phil and I drove north to the city of Munising, a town on the shores of Lake Superior.

The very first National Lakeshore designated in America was this stretch of Lake Superior shoreline, Pictured Rocks. Sandstone cliffs line the lake here, rising over 200 feet in places. Water oozing through the rock carries minerals with it that "paint" the cliffs. Iron streaks the sandstone red and orange, copper smudges it blue and green, manganese leaves black marks, and lime highlights the rocks with white smears. The cliffs have also eroded into interesting shapes: arches and caves and a series of chunky walls butting out into the water.

Seismic disruptions helped to form Lake Superior, which is why it is so much deeper than the other Great Lakes. In fact, Lake Superior holds more water than the other four Great Lakes combined. The lake stays cold because of its immense size and depth, and this influences the weather around its shores. There are arctic plants that thrive near the lake due to the cool and moist zones there. The thimbleberry and arctic crowberry are two such plants that are normally found much further north.

I was delighted that we had a gorgeous, sunny day to enjoy the boat ride along this national treasure.

My second day off was spent tracking down a new pair of boots. The rock and brush of the UP had shredded the pair I'd been wearing. I had hoped they would get me to the city of Green Bay, but when a lace loop broke on the last day, I inspected the other loops to find that were also failing, then inspected the soles. Several of the air-filled treads were now worn completely open, exposing the air cavity. I probably should have switched to a more rugged boot for the UP, but these had worked well until they gave out. After making a few phone calls, I found a store in Escanaba with boots and I wore them the rest of the day to break them in a bit before beginning the trek south to Green Bay.

Segment 8

But it's a WET heat!

I camped my way south of Escanaba for several days, so this meant carrying a heavier pack. I wasn't worried about the weight this time, because the previous 663 miles had toughened me up considerably, but when I heard that the highs would be in the 80s, I was concerned. I could handle the cold when hiking, but tended – especially with a large pack – to overheat when it got hot.

One trick I'd learn to help me stay cool was to wet a bandana and wrap it around my neck. An improvement on that was to take the wet ends and loop them over my ears. This, surprisingly, had a noticeable effect on how I felt in the heat. Human ears are not known for regulating body heat as much as those of rabbits and elephants, but having the water evaporate off my ears must have improved the efficiency of "ear heat transfer."

I took several photos of myself, hoping that the bandana looked like it was tied to the arms on my glasses (or something), but, no. I looked like a dork with a wet bandana looped over her ears. Since it was working to keep me cool, I kept doing it, dorky or not. I waved goodbye to Phil in Escanaba and began walking south on Highway 35.

Since the lake level was still on the low side, Green Bay was also low. The bay tends to be shallow anyway. Along much of the shoreline, wetland plants grow in the shallows and out into the bay. Sometimes, there was a strip of sand where the beach used to be when the water was much higher, but now there was a swampy strip instead between the sand and open water.

Once I left Escanaba, I knew I wouldn't encounter many commercial establishments; there were only campgrounds, one gas station and one bar for the next 50 miles. The bar and gas station – the only places with food along the way – were within sight of each other near the Cedar River.

Hiking south, I could soon see Washington Island, then the Door Peninsula 15 miles across Green Bay. The gap between the island and tip of the peninsula is called Death's Door, a name, one thinks, that must have been earned. Many a vessel – from native canoes to schooners – came to a tragic end in this six-mile-wide passage with its treacherous currents and rocky shallows. I had considered hiking a route that included the length of the beautiful Door Peninsula, but had opted for the more contiguous hike on the western shore of Green Bay. Looking across the calm bay waters, I longed to be hiking on the hilly peninsula where I could appreciate both the bay and the waters of the Great Lake.

A couple of times I was able to make forays to the shoreline, at places like Bailey Park, and at boat launches. Bailey Park seemed to have had a nice beach at one time, but marsh grasses had grown between the sand and the water like a massive green wall. It was nice to walk on sand along this stretch, though, and to hear the wind rustling the poplars and grasses instead of the cars and many trucks on Highway 35.

My camping experiences were pleasant, despite a thunderstorm the first night. Being in a hammock tent suspended between two trees, I wondered what would happen if lightening struck either of the trees. I tried not to dwell on this and got a decent night's sleep that first night nestled in the woods.

The second night I stopped at Kleinke Park. All the other occupied spaces there had house-sized campers. It was comical to walk the row of numbered sites on the bay and see: house-camper, house-camper, house-camper, hammock-tent-suspended-between-two-trees, house-camper, house-camper. People at Kleinke were very kind, and two couples adopted me for a dinner of grilled steak and veggies and a fresh salad. It was worlds better than the granola and jerky I had planned to eat.

The two couples had been camping there for many years. "Ten years ago, we'd take our boat just off the shore there," one of the women pointed, "and catch our limit of perch in a matter of an hour or so."

"And now?" I asked.

"Now, all we catch are round goby," one of the men answered.

The other man said they were so aggressive that you could catch them using a bare hook.

First spotted in the St. Clair River in 1990, in less than two decades the fish have invaded and established themselves in all the Great Lakes. In Milwaukee, they've started raising perch in massive tanks in an old warehouse to meet the demand for the fish commonly used in Friday night fish fries. Lake Michigan, it seems, is no longer a safe place for perch.

One of the couples had two daughters working that summer on the Door Peninsula across the bay. There were many summer jobs there because it was a popular tourist destination, and their girls worked for one of the boat companies that gave tours. Our conversation about their daughters made me miss my sons. I had thought of them often, and had recently spoken to Lucas, but these three weeks would be the longest I had ever gone without seeing either one of them.

The final state: Wisconsin

From Kleinke, I walked to the city of Menominee, on the banks of the Menominee River, and explored the historic waterfront. This town also had an era of prosperity linked to the lumbering boom of the late 1800s. There were still deposits of wood and sawdust in the shallow water off the marina and along the beach.

The Menominee River is the boundary between the western edge of Michigan's Upper Peninsula and the state of Wisconsin. I stopped in the middle of the bridge, at the point where Michigan ended and Wisconsin began. I took a moment to realize that I was entering the last state on my trek along the lake.

Along the way to the city of Peshtigo, the heavens opened and poured rain down on me for over an hour. I had to pass a huge construction zone where they were draining a large tract of wetlands, trucking in tons of dirt, and building a new highway. At some points, they had planted wheat along the shoulder of the road to stabilize the fresh earth. It was strange to see the golden sheaves of wheat waving in the wind alongside the heavy equipment that tore at the land.

From Peshtigo, I pushed south toward Oconto. Along the way, I met up with a man on a bicycle going the opposite direction. He was a chubby guy with a graying beard that flared out from his jaw line like he had been frightened. He wore brown shorts and a gray tank top that had lines of salt from his dried sweat.

He coasted to a stop and asked me where I was going. When I told him about my adventure, he began telling me all about the area. Karl ("With a 'K,' like Karl Marx," he said) told me about the Peshtigo Fire which had happened on the same day as the Great Chicago Fire in October of 1871. The Peshtigo Fire burned over a million acres of forest, sweeping across the land like a fiery cyclone, and took around 2,000 lives. Community records were destroyed in the fire and, in many places, there were no survivors to remember the dead, so the death toll isn't exact.

"The Chicago fire gets all the press," he said, "but sometimes they remember Peshtigo, too. It was bigger, you know, but there were fewer people up here to witness it. Most of the people who saw the fire were burned up."

Karl also told me about a time in the 1980s when the lake level was so high that they had to use snow plows in the middle of summer to remove debris that would come up onto the streets of Oconto after storms. He talked about the highway they were constructing that I had passed through and the folly of filling in the wetlands there.

"Wetlands are necessary. Are highways?" he asked before pedaling away.

Fascination with roadkill

I have a confession to make: all along the Lake Trek, I had taken many photos of roadkill and dead creatures on the lakeshore. As morbid as this may seem, it arose from the boredom I felt while walking through Gary, Indiana, where I began taking photos of interesting roadside trash. Gary is the hands-down capital of interesting trash. Single gloves of all sorts are often along the road, as are single shoes.

The one time I saw a pair of work boots on the side of the road, it was unsettling. If you see one shoe, you think, "someone lost their shoe." If you see both of them, you wonder what horrible fate happened to the person wearing them, especially in Gary.

The most interesting grouping that I had seen in Gary was a woman's furry high-heel boot, curly hair extensions, and a dead cat. That made for quite a photo and constructing a story around that creepy tableau – involving a hooker and her abusive cat pimp whom she eventually killed – occupied my twisted mind for several miles of otherwise boring roadside walking.

Some of the other interesting pieces of trash I had seen elsewhere were a broken coconut with all the meat still inside, sitting on a beach in Indiana (lost from some drink-making mishap on a boat?) and a very nice of pair of men's leather Cole Haan shoes placed as if on display (one shoe propped rakishly atop the other) on a roadside phone junction box near Harbor Springs. That town was so upscale that even their roadside trash had a designer label.

But back to the dead animals. When driving by roadkill, I feel a small pang of regret for their lack of timing. When I walked by these dead animals, however, the experience was more personal. Often, I could see the anguish on their dead faces. Not imagined anguish, but real, eye-popping, tongue-lolling, little-arms-extending-in-pain anguish. I began taking photographs, I guess as a way to document their lives and, if they had been run over, their manmade death.

Up to this point in northern Wisconsin, I had seen tens of dead deer, many squirrel, raccoon, possum, rabbit and badgers, a bushel of small birds (including three hummingbirds, a blue bird, and one wren), one very large bird (a blue heron), two shrew, two bats, two rats, one fox, quite a few turtles and frogs, lots of porcupine and several unidentifiable mash-ups of bone and fur.

At one point, I saw the severed head of a porcupine. The body was nowhere in sight.

The lakeshore was not without its share of carcasses. There were, of course, hundreds of dead fish of all species – or just their picked-clean vertebrae – washed up on the sand and rocks. From shiny alewives to gutted salmon, an occasional whiskered carp or round goby, and one sharp-toothed muskie, these deaths fed the gulls and shore animals. I saw many deer, turtle, dead and dying waterfowl of all types – ducks, gulls, cormorants (many ingest plastic or lead weights and die, some contract avian botulism), and two drowning victims: a squirrel and a possum. Both their little faces looked rather surprised, like they had been pushed.

I got to the point where I could smell the roadkill and estimate –before seeing the carcass – what state of decay I would find. I saw a freshly killed doe whose last thrashings had flattened a circle of still green grass around her, her eyes wide in disbelief. I saw deer carcass several days old on which predators had feasted. I saw skeletons of deer long dead, picked clean by birds and beasts and bugs, scattered around like a puzzle; the sun bleaching each bone brilliant white.

It was along the stretch between Peshtigo and Oconto, however, that I saw the most heartbreaking roadkill. The first was a great horned owl. It must have fractured its skull or broken its neck on impact because it didn't have a mark on it, not a drop of blood anywhere. I was hopeful that maybe it was only stunned, but as I moved its wing, I felt that it was beginning to stiffen in death. One wing was outstretched, the other folded against its body, its eyelids – which close from the bottom up – were mostly shut, leaving just a sliver of the golden-rimmed eyeball exposed.

This is a magnificent bird, and it was both fascinating to see it so close and heartbreaking to know it was dead. I studied its long, sharp, curved black talons on the end of its feathered feet. I'm sure it was horrifying for the driver to have this massive bird bounce off his windshield in the middle of the night, but I couldn't help feeling far more sorry for the owl.

As I gently moved the owl from the rocky shoulder of the road into the tall weeds nearby, I worked my fingers through its downy belly feathers. I closed my eyes and imagined how it was to fly as this bird of prey through the night sky, to hear the *woomp woomp* of great wings flapping in the cool night air, to see with night vision the prey that would be its next warm meal.

As I nestled it gently in the tall grass, I was astonished by how little it weighed.

It was only a mile or so from the owl that I saw my first (and only) dead lynx on the road. Both the bobcat and lynx are making a comeback in the more remote sections around the lake – I had seen some sort of small cat prints near a dead deer on the beach on the other side of the lake – but I had never caught a glimpse of the cats themselves until this sad moment.

It's strange to consider roadkill this way, but these animals bespoke of a great biodiversity around Green Bay. It took a stable and diverse food web to support two large predators. I hoped that the demise of these two on the roads wasn't a negative indicator for the future of their species in the area.

Vickie doesn't run me over

As I walk south toward the city of Oconto, I call my friend Vickie. When she first heard about my Lake Trek, she was excited and vowed to be part of it. "All I need," she told me, "is my passport and a gun permit." Now, many people had asked me what part of the Lake Trek has been the scariest. I always answer that it is the thought of Vickie with a gun. After telling her that she wouldn't need her passport because Lake Michigan was the only Great Lake within the borders of the U.S., I tried to dissuade her from following up on the gun permit.

Now, as she's driving from southern Indiana up to Wisconsin to shuttle me around the bottom of the bay for several days, I wonder if she'll be packing heat. We talk on the phone, trying to determine how far apart we are as she makes her way north toward me. I walk to the end of a construction zone and wait there as cars emerge from one lane back and accelerate back to two.

As I wait, I notice that the shoulder is made up of loose, white rocks, and that it slants toward a deep, water-filled ditch. I think about how Vickie might pull off the road, then brake as she approaches me. How the little rocks might slide around. I try to remember if the front of her Jeep has that special bar on it that I might grab onto, or if leaping down into the ditch might be the best option.

As I contemplate my choices, I see her emerge from the construction zone. I wave and she pulls over. Her tires make a gravel-slipping sound. I take two quick steps back and tense to jump, but she grinds the vehicle to a halt as her car bumper nudges against my leg. Relieved, I walk to the passenger side and open the door.

Vickie is smiling. "I was thinking on the way up that I'd probably run you over when I finally found you!"

I burst into laughter. "I was thinking the same thing! I almost jumped into the ditch!"

After being on my own for so many days, it is great to see a friend. We settle into our hotel rooms, then have a nice dinner that first night and catch up. Vickie tells everyone we encounter about my Lake Trek.

"She's walking all the way around Lake Michigan," she says, pointing at me. "Isn't that amazing?"

The next day, she shuttled me back to Oconto and I walked south to Green Bay over the next two days. As I got closer to the city, the shoreline became a thick wetland with many small streams and rivers. There were two access points to the bay along this stretch where I hiked out hoping to see the water.

The first was a wildlife area in Pensaukee. It was a swath of wetlands with one mown pathway. Tall marsh grasses grew up on either side to well over my head, and knee high on the path itself. As I approached the bay, the path got muckier, and I scared up some ducks from a puddle. I saw deer tracks and places where they had bedded down in the grass. I saw skins shed by snakes, tiny toads that could balance on the tip of my finger, and flustered grouse. The grass got even taller by the bay until it was an eight-foot wall preventing my progress.

The second place where I could access the bay was the L. H. Barkhausen Waterfowl Preserve outside of Suamico. They have a lovely interpretive center with many preserved wildlife specimens, and I thought back to that magnificent dead owl and wished I had known about the place. There were trails that wound through the over 900 acres.

Since it was mostly wetlands, swarms of mosquitoes also had a wonderful habitat. My hike through the area turned into a jog because of them, but it was great to be off the road and near the water. I saw ducks, rabbits, and thousands of mosquitoes. This preserve has an 8-acre marsh where the northern pike return to spawn each year.

The 750-mile mark

It was south of the preserve that I reached the 750-mile mark in my trek. I was on a road that headed straight for the bay, then curved south again. I paused on that curve and looked at the undulating wall of marsh grasses, then I looked south and could see the industry of the city of Green Bay in the hazy distance.

While a city like Chicago has preserved its relationship with the lakeshore with parks and paths, Green Bay had industrialized its waterfront, then lofted a highway over the top of it. While I was elated to have reached the 3/4 milestone in my trek, I was missing Lake Michigan. Green Bay was too calm, too shallow, too marshy to give me the sandy shorelines I longed to be walking.

It was, however, a fantastic place for waterfowl, and the bay and rivers feeding into it were a rich source of life connected to the lake. I knew that many birds followed the Fox River up into the bay when migrating. Early settlers around Green Bay reported that flocks of birds would block the sun due to their numbers.

I longed to be a duck to fully appreciate the beauty from above and while paddling with webbed feet in the lush marshes.

I was getting a little homesick, having been away for almost three weeks. While I had chatted with Jim (who by now actually seemed to be excited about my progress) and Lucas, I had not spoken to Ben since saying goodbye to him on the docks of Mackinac Island. He was doing a summer study in Germany. Lucas had a piano recital at the end of his camp that I wanted to make, though, so I put in several 20-mile days in order to get home in time.

When I had reached the 500-mile mark, I still had the entire UP ahead of me. I had a mixture of accomplishment for what I had done and trepidation about what stretched out before me. At the 750-mile mark, I thought that the toughest terrain was behind me, and that the miles remaining would not be as wild and remote as the ones already covered.

I also felt stronger in my body and in my skills to move through the land. Fifteen pounds had dropped off me to be replaced by hard muscle. I had been rained on, blown over, splashed by waves; I had climbed up bluffs and through dunes and over rock walls; I had sloshed through marshes, waded creeks, and extracted myself from soggy bogs and primordial forests. I had doubled back when presented with an obstacle and continued another way forward.

So much had been thrown at me, but, even when exhausted and sweaty and hungry, I had gotten to the end of the day, the end of the miles, the end of a segment. The 750-mile mark was a moment to think about how the trek had changed and shaped me.

The idea of walking another 250 miles almost seemed like an easy thing to do, but I had no idea how tough the terrain would be in the coming miles, or how my body would rebel against me at the most crucial point of all.

A toxic legacy

From that milestone, I walked all the way into the city of Green Bay and crossed over the Fox River. This river was once one of the most polluted draining into the Great Lakes. It still boasts the highest concentrations of paper mills in the world: 24 mills on less than 40 miles of river. There have been some efforts to clean up the Fox River in the last decade, and a new nine-year effort had started in 2009. This project will "dredge and cap" over 30 miles of the river and its mouth where it joins Green Bay. This process involves collecting the top layer of river sediment, processing it into toxic "cakes" where most of the PCBs are concentrated, dumping these into a special landfill, then capping the dredged river with unpolluted sand and gravel to prevent remaining toxins from moving in the river.

Over the several days that Vickie and I stayed at the hotel, we established a routine. While I hiked, Vickie worked on preparing for the classes she was teaching in the fall. When I had finished for the day, I'd take a shower, then head down to the pool to let the jets in the hot tub work on my calf muscles. Then, I'd get ready for dinner. Vickie and I would go out to eat, trying places around Green Bay, including Curly's Pub at the famous Lambeau Field where the Packers play. Green Bay holds the proud distinction of being the smallest city to have an NFL franchise, and the city feels like it is oriented toward the stadium, perpetually cheering on the Packers.

Curly's Pub was named as the most "Green Bay-y" place to eat in Green Bay. Outside the stadium, there are two massive bronze sculptures on tall pedestals: one of the famous Packers coach, Vince Lombardi, and one of Packers founder and coach for the team's first 30 years, Curly Lambeau.

As Vickie and I approach the statues, we notice a couple with a yellow Labrador retriever. The dog is freaked out by the giant, bronze men and barks crazily at them. The woman holding the dog's leash is cracking up at the inanity of the situation. The husband smiles at them. The woman is laughing so hard that tears stream down her face. She tries, occasionally, to say something reassuring to the dog – that they are statues, not real metal men – but the dog barks insistently at them on their tall pedestals. This cracks up the woman even more.

Her husband eventually puts his arm around her, takes the leash of the crazed dog, and leads them both – still barking dog and still laughing woman – away from the stadium.

Inside, Vickie and I follow the signs upstairs to Curly's Pub. We take seats near a window so we can look out over the city. I try to order the most Green Bay-y thing and choose a brat boiled in beer then topped with sauerkraut. Vickie orders the Wisconsin cheese soup and a salad.

Vickie had recently found out that one of her novels had won a contest and would be published the next year. During the time when she was a finalist, we had met for lunch and had walked through a bookstore together.

"I swear," she said, "if I don't win this contest, I'm going to write one of these bodice-rippers." She held up a book where a woman, indeed, was having her bodice ripped by a bare-chested, muscular man.

"Come on," I said, "there are too many of those already."

"There are lots of these because they get published. Literary fiction doesn't get published, so what good is it?"

"Okay, fine. You'll probably write better sex scenes than they do anyway," I said.

Now, months later, she had learned that her book would be published and we were eating Green Bay-y food in Green Bay. "How did you celebrate?" I ask. "When you learned about the publishing contract?"

"We've been so busy," she says, then she tears up a bit. "I don't think it's sunk in yet."

"Hey, we're celebrating now. I'm so jazzed for you! You should be proud." Vickie is a self-deprecating woman and she seems to struggle with embracing the win.

"Well, it's nice to be with another writer. You know how hard it is, at least. Not everyone understands why we keep writing."

"Why is that again?" I joke.

"Because we're masochists, I guess."

I had planned two days to walk across the base of the Door Peninsula from Green Bay to Manitowoc. It made sense to have Vickie drop me in the middle of the peninsula both days. The first day, I'd hike back to Green Bay, the second I'd hike to Manitowoc. Denmark, Wisconsin, was the town nearest the middle of the peninsula.

The first day, I walked a path that was a "rails-to-trails" project. There is a movement all over the country to take unused railroad lines and convert them into hiking and biking trails. The one running through Denmark is the Devils River State Recreation Trail. The path did not extend very far toward Green Bay, so I continued on the old railroad line.

Walking a railroad is mesmerizing. I had to keep my eyes on the wooden ties because they were uneven and spaced in a way that did not match my stride. By this point in the trek, I often had the sensation that the world was turning beneath me, that I was almost hovering above it while it moved underneath my boots. The railroad ties streaming beneath me heightened this effect. Walking had become automatic and almost effortless.

The southern end of the Door Peninsula is largely farm country. There are rolling fields of corn and hay and large dairy farms. In the town of Ledgeview, the land lifts and I was treated to a sweeping view of the city of Green Bay and beyond. I crossed the Fox River at De Pere and stopped to watch the white pelicans and many ducks by the paper factory that hovers over the river. I heard that long ago, mill workers used to bring their shot-guns to work during duck season so they could hunt on their lunch break.

On the final day of this segment, Vickie dropped me back in Denmark. She strolled with me for a little bit, then we hugged and parted. She headed back to her home in Indiana, and I hiked toward the city of Manitowoc on the shores of Lake Michigan.

The Devils River Trail was complete for several miles heading south-east. They had either removed the rails, or had topped them with a thick layer of crushed stone. At the beginning, the trail was wide and smooth, but then it transitioned into a weedy two-track a-bloom with Queen Anne's lace and thistle. I continued on this for several more miles until the trail disappeared into a field.

I continued on roads until I found another section of completed trail near the town of Maribel. I passed the town's granary and stopped in at a gas station for a cold drink. Their sign advertised "cooler treats, baler twine, and fly tape."

From there the trail was smooth and ramrod straight for miles, passing through dense, mossy woods and verdant farmland with enormous wooden barns perched atop limestone foundations. I heard the buzzing of high-voltage power lines overhead along the way, the crashing of startled deer through the woods, and the whisper of flapping geese wings as they flew overhead in formation.

A light sprinkle of rain made even the air smell green.

Finally, back to my lake

Long before I reached the city of Manitowoc, I saw its massive, light-blue water tower painted with the name of the city and a ship's wheel. By the time I got to the city and crossed over the river and then made it out to the harbor, I had hiked the longest day of the trek, 25 miles. Not even the physical toll of hiking 25 miles with my heavy pack could stop me from feeling elated at seeing Lake Michigan. I strolled along the harbor to feel the wind off the lake, to smell the clean, lake smell.

I was headed home for some rest and relaxation. I had booked night passage on the Badger Car Ferry that crosses from Manitowoc to Ludington, Michigan. The steam ship, launched in 1952, still runs on coal and measures over 400 feet long and almost 60 feet wide. It used to transport railroad cars across the lake. Now it takes cars and buses and – as I watched it unload the passengers and their vehicles – I realized that it even transported houses. A large tractor trailer towing a massive mobile home pulled off the boat in Manitowoc.

From the upper deck around midnight, I watched the last of the vehicles drive into the hold. Then, a deckhand gave the signal to lower the massive, black sea-gate, an apron of steel that protects the rear of the boat. I had read about these railroad ferryboats and had learned about one whose sea-gate had not locked into the lowered position. This allowed water to rush into the hold during a violent storm. The ship still rests at the bottom of the lake.

I had hoped to see the stars from the boat, but a thick fog had formed as the day cooled. It was haunting to move through the mist with the boat's steam engine thrumming beneath my boots, having no sense of where we were in the dark. The lake was rather calm, so that massive boat felt suspended in space and time. I had booked a tiny cabin, so I stashed my pack and walking stick and walked the decks for an hour, happy to be out on the lake again. Then, I settled in for a couple hours sleep.

After waking, I watched as the lights of Ludington Harbor appeared in the fog. Our ship called out into the darkness with its massive horn and the foghorn in Ludington answered. The boat docked at 5:30 a.m.

My shipmates and I staggered off the boat back in the state of Michigan, tired and a little dazed in the dark, the foghorn still calling out in the mist.

.

Segment 9

August 26–30
Manitowoc to Milwaukee
91 miles in 5 days

Total Trek Mileage: 911 miles

Between 8 and 9

I had 33 days off between Segments 8 and 9. This was my longest break during the Lake Trek. It was certainly deserved and desired after hiking 316 miles in the back-to-back segments along the southern edge of Michigan's Upper Peninsula, along Green Bay, and across the Door Peninsula to Manitowoc. But it was also strange to be away from the lake for so long.

There was a stretch of lakeshore that I had not explored on Segment 2 when Ben hiked with me. A nuclear power plant had diverted us inland and over the highway. By the time we could cross back to the lake, we were at our stopping point for the day. The feature I had missed was Grand Mere State Park. During this long break, I returned to visit this park south of Stevensville, Michigan.

Grand Mere State Park is unique in that you must leave your car in the woods and hike over dunes to the lake. There are two inland lakes there – kettle lakes – that were formed when giant chunks of ice broke free from the retreating glacier thousands of years ago. The massive pieces of ice fell from near the top of the glacier and stuck deep into the ground. Over time, wind pushed sand and soil around the edges of the ice, and when the ice melted it filled the deep depression with fresh, glacial water.

I hiked alongside one of these ancient lakes. It was surrounded by mature trees and looked primordial. Then, I left the cool of the woods and hiked over the dunes and out to Lake Michigan.

This August day was much warmer than when Ben and I hiked this segment in March. Lake Michigan was deep blue out where it reflected the sky, and turquoise near the shore where the choppy, shallow water refracted the light differently. I walked the shoreline for about a mile. The park protects nearly 1,000 acres, and birders frequent the area during spring and fall migrations. Since this area has such unique geological features, it has been designated a National Natural Landmark.

On the way home, I stopped at the Wolf Lake Fish Hatchery west of Kalamazoo. This hatchery is the only one to raise lake sturgeon. They have a large tank in the visitor's center filled with finger-length sturgeon. This ancient species of fish can grow up to six feet long, so it was strange to see them in miniature. There are a series of DNR hatcheries – six in the state of Michigan alone – that grow up and then "plant" fish in both inland lakes and the Great Lakes.

The ecosystem of the Great Lakes is very man-manipulated. I often thought about this while walking the lakeshore. I wished we could just magically restore the ecosystem back to when it was last in balance, which was probably in the mid-1800s. This, unfortunately, is impossible. Some of the fish that populated the Great Lakes then are now extinct. Inland riverbanks needed for natural spawning have been so denuded and eroded or developed that they can never be restored to the wild way they once were. And there's no way to completely eradicate the invasive species that have invaded the Great Lakes.

The condition of the lakes today is the starting point for restoration efforts; there is no going back to a long-ago ideal. There is a plan to address some of these problems, it is called the Great Lakes Restoration Initiative (GLRI). The year I was making my way around the lake, this legislation was making its way through Congress. The EPA held meetings to get input from communities and organizations involved in watching over the lakes. I went to one of these gatherings in Lansing during my long break.

The GLRI targets five issues: toxic substances, combating invasive species, nearshore health and nonpoint source pollution, habitat and wildlife protection and restoration, and accountability (including evaluation, communication, and partnerships). The plan is to fund the effort at the level of $5 billion spread out over ten years.

The meeting I attended had over 250 attendees representing such diverse organizations as Ducks Unlimited, the Alliance for the Great Lakes, Kalamazoo Watershed Council, and the Saginaw Valley Convention and Visitors Bureau. There were also government officials, including Mayor Hartwell of Grand Rapids and staffers from some of Michigan's Congressional members. There were also a handful of people who just love the lakes.

The GRLI comes with a well-developed plan on how to channel these funds. It was encouraging to hear Cameron Davis from the EPA talk about swimming in Lake Michigan with his kids before he talked about policy. With the complex problems facing the Great Lakes, it will take a concerted and well-funded initiative like this to move toward improving the health of our lakes.

Back on the Lake Trek

There is a high-speed car ferry that crosses Lake Michigan between Muskegon, Michigan, and Milwaukee, Wisconsin, a distance of nearly 100 miles of blue water that takes the catamaran only 2 ½ hours. Since Phil was going to shadow me on this segment, I booked passage for my car, too. After driving into the hold and setting the parking brake, Phil and I climbed up to the top deck to watch as the boat left Muskegon Lake and headed through a channel to Lake Michigan.

The lake was choppy with waves up to 5 feet, and the catamaran accelerated as we passed the channel markers. Phil and I descended to the middle deck and claimed some chairs near a window. The crossing was a little rough, especially when one side of the boat fell into a deep trough between waves.

I ventured onto the upper deck in the middle of the lake. With the 35-mph speed of the boat added to the 10- to 20-mph headwinds it was difficult to stand, let alone move around the deck. I worried that if I turned my head just right, the wind would fling my glasses into the lake. I clung to the railings as I made my way back to the passenger deck and took my seat next to Phil.

He looked at my wild hair. "Little windy?"

I smoothed my hair and straightened my glasses on my nose.

"What makes you ask?" I deadpanned.

There were high, hazy clouds in the sky, and the lake was the color of worn denim, the whitecaps frays in the fabric. In the middle of the lake there was water in all directions. I expected to see a whale breach, a lake monster surface, or at least a school of enormous salmon jumping in unison, but it was all water: moving, rolling, endless to the eye.

My first day back in Wisconsin on the Lake Trek felt good. I wanted to move, to walk, to feel the sand roll beneath me. When I finally left the city streets of Manitowoc and headed to the shoreline, though, I was greeted with the largest *cladophora* algae bloom I had ever seen.

This algae is native to the Great Lakes, but has been growing out-of-control lately. Run-off carrying fertilizer and animal waste from farms, cities dumping sewage during heavy rains, and seepage from septic tanks along the shoreline feed these blooms. The result, along this first day of Segment 9, was a thick mat of dead and dying algae along the shoreline, and a floating mat stretching out into the lake as far as 30 feet at times.

It was a warm day, so the rotting algae smelled horrible. It was even blooming in the streams emptying into the lake. Tire-sized algae mats floated slowly into the lake to meld with the heaps of algae there. I passed several signs along the shore warning about the poor water quality and advising against swimming.

Then I saw a sign about Viral Hemorrhagic Syndrome. This virus has been found in fish in the area (kind of like a fish Ebola plague that causes them to bleed all over). As I walked, I was convinced it was time to address what is going horribly wrong with the lake.

The algae presented me with a more immediate problem – my drinking water came from the lake. This algae would have clogged the filters in my bottle, though, so I couldn't dip into the lake like I had done for hundreds of miles.

I considered wading out past the thickest of the bloom, but then I would have been covered with sticky algae.

Thankfully, some small streams emerged from the sand and clay bluffs and trickled their way to the lake. These were either spring fed, or came from places where the water table was above lake level. Either way, the water was cold and at least partially filtered by passing through the sand.

Fast talker, fast walker

An old college friend of mine, Stephanie, flew from North Carolina to Milwaukee to join me for the remaining days of this segment. We had been emailing for months about how she should train and what gear she should bring. We had dinner together that first night, and she caught me up on her life since I'd last seen her over 15 years earlier.

Stephanie is six feet tall, blond, and a world-class fast-talker. She said more words during that dinner than I say in a week. We had many years to cover, though, so it was good that she could move through them so quickly.

I had given her the nickname of "Stew" in college because she was incredibly, militantly frugal. At Calvin College, the school we attended, there was a philosophy of stewardship; that is, a way of living where one is responsible toward caring for the environment. She was the best steward I had ever met, so I shortened it to "Stew" for her.

I once saw her retrieve a sliver of soap from the trash and put it in a piece of an old panty hose. Curious – and a little alarmed – I asked her what she was up to. "A few more and I'll have a new bar of soap," she said. She continued collecting cast-off soaps, tied off the panty hose, and, indeed, soon had a strange-looking, grayish green, mutant soap bar.

The environment has always been important to me, but I didn't mind parting with a sliver of soap when I could see through it. Stew, however, saw the value in everything.

The first day with Stew began quite early. I had received permission from the Whistling Straits Golf Course to walk the edge of their lakeshore course. This course is a world-class site designed in the style of the rugged seaside courses of Scotland. The photos on their website indeed brought to mind Scotland with its rolling hills and rocky shore. In one photo, there were even sheep grazing in the rough.

The catch, the course manager said, was that we had to begin before the first tee time. We got up early, dressed and gulped some coffee. Phil dropped us off where another Calvin graduate who lived in the area, Lois, was waiting for us in the morning mist. She was a few years ahead of us, so we hadn't known her in college. She was a very fit-looking woman with short blond hair, and she broke into an easy grin when we got out of the car.

Quite a few people had emailed offering to meet up with me to walk, and I tried to coordinate with them. Often, I learned a lot about "their" stretch of the lakeshore and how it had changed over the years or what challenges were facing the lake near them. Sometimes I got to hear great stories about the history of an area or current events in their town, or, like with Rick and Mary, sadder tales of toxic disregard for the lake.

Lois had been on long hikes before and is quite comfortable scrambling along the shore of the golf course with Stew and me.

"Are there really sheep here?" I ask. "Or was that just for the website photos?"

"No. They graze here all the time," she answers. "My son works summers as a groundskeeper here."

Stew smiles. "Great job."

"I've never walked the lake up here since we live right by the Kohler-Andrae Park," Lois says, pausing to look down on the lake. "It's close, and it's all sandy beach. You'll walk through that tomorrow, I guess. I didn't know the bluff was so high here."

After we cover the two miles the golf course has along the lake, we walk through the edge of several acres of woods on the bluff. "I think this is a nature preserve," Lois says.

Then we walk along the edge of some farmland planted with tall corn and lush soybeans. We cut inland along the soybean field to get Lois back to where she had left her car.

A small plane swoops over the cornfield, spraying the crops. He passes low over the corn, then catches an updraft off the lake bluff which he uses to lift and turn the plane. It looks like great fun, but then he turns and buzzes low over us.

"Wow, I feel like we're in North by Northwest," I say to blank looks from Stew and Lois. "Hitchcock movie? Cary Grant?" Still blank. "He's running through a cornfield and a plane swoops down at him?" Nothing. Apparently not everyone is a Hitchcock fan. We press on out to the road.

Stew and I say goodbye to Lois, then make our way down the bluff to the rocky shore and continue at the waterline. We pass more *cladophora* along this stretch, but only in patches and not like the thick mat I had seen the day before. The shoreline is rugged in places, with downed trees at the water's edge, often forcing us into the brush to find the nearest deer trail to walk.

At Sheboygan we cut inland and into town for lunch. I rarely stopped for lunch, but it was a welcome break during this tough day of hiking. Lois had suggested we try a restaurant on the Sheboygan River, and Stew and I had a pleasant break while sitting outside on the riverfront. Sheboygan has an enormous lakefront power plant just to the south, so leaving town we stay inland until we were well past it and the containment pools for the coal ash.

The second day that Stew is with me is the easiest day of the segment: the stretch between two state parks, the Kohler-Andrae and Harrington. The 14 miles between them is generally sandy and wide and easy to walk. Stew decides to wear her hiking sandals since her boots are giving her blisters.

During this day, we see rain showers out on the lake or south of us, but we never have a drop fall on us. Toward the end of the day, we see an elderly couple watching over their young granddaughters as they catch frogs in a small stream near their beach house. The older girl is putting her catch into a large cooler, and I ask if we can see her captives.

As we approach, the grandfather looks at our backpacks, smiles and asks, "What are you doing, walkin' to Chicago?"

When Stew points to me and says, "She is," his mouth drops open. I tell him about the Lake Trek.

"Ten years ago, I thought I'd bike around Lake Michigan," he says. "Haven't gotten to it."

"This is my year with the lake," I say. "I didn't want to wait any longer."

His wife explains that the frog project had started back in the spring when the girls would catch tadpoles, study them, then put them back. This ongoing catch-and-release program is now into late summer and the tadpoles had sprouted legs, sucked in their tails, and turned into beautiful, black-eyed leopard frogs, their strong legs cocked, ready to unfurl.

The girls are expert frog-catchers. This is a skill I prided myself on as a young girl (along with snake-, grasshopper-, praying mantis-, and any other creature-catcher). For many years when my sons were young, I had collected praying mantis egg cases so we could watch them hatch in the spring. I'd sew some thread through the spongy case to suspend it in a large canning jar, which we'd keep on the kitchen counter. One day, without fanfare, the baby mantises would begin lowering themselves from the egg case on threads of silk. Then they'd unfurl to reveal perfectly formed, miniature mantises. Usually, over a hundred would rappel from a single egg case.

We'd also waded in many streams, catching tadpoles and frogs and crayfish and baby turtles. It seems like this fascination with nature has been replaced by video games with today's kids, so I am happy to see these fearless frog hunters wading the shallows for their quarry.

The older girl comes up to me with something in her hand. She opens it slightly.

"It's a toad," she says.

I look into her little hand at the bumpy back of the small toad. "You know how to tell it apart from the frogs?"

"Yep. That's easy," she says as she lets the toad go and returns to hunting the shallows.

Stew and I say goodbye to the young frog hunters and continue walking the wide beach toward our ending point for the day, Harrington Beach State Park. One of the last houses along this day's hike is owned by a couple who also graduated from Calvin College, Milt and Carol. They had contacted me earlier and are waiting on the beach to greet us. They rise from their lawn chairs and give a wave as we approach, then invite us inside. There, they graciously serve us cold drinks, and we settle into soft chairs.

"You have a lovely spot here so near the park," Stew says.

"We call that our side yard," Milt jokes. "We take our grandkids fishing on that little lake inside the park."

A worried look passes over Carol's face. "As long as they wear their lifejackets, of course."

"It's quite deep," Milt adds. "It's quarried down about sixty feet. Have you seen it?"

"Tomorrow we'll hike through there," I say.

"They mined limestone, then they cooked it in a kiln over there," Milt points through the wall of his house. "They used it to make cement."

"Portland cement?" I ask.

"I think that's right," Carol says. "Immigrants from Luxembourg worked there. That's why the nearby town is called Belgium."

"Isn't Luxembourg its own tiny country?" I ask.

"I think it was ruled by Belgium for a time," she says.

The conversation turns to the lake, how it rises and falls from year to year, its beauty, and to how it feels to walk almost all the way around it.

Wisconsin food

Stew, as I mentioned, is a six-foot tall blond. It's easy to pick her out in a crowd, especially when she's smiling. Once, during college, I was canoeing with her in the middle of nowhere with only one other boat on the lake. The people in the other boat recognized her from a long distance and yelled out her name. It was no surprise that she knew people along this stretch of Wisconsin.

Stew's husband's cousin, Dave, lives north of Milwaukee, and he met up with us one night to take us out to get Wisconsin food.

"So glad to meet you," Dave says as we shake hands. He looks a lot like Stew's husband, Ray: medium height, warm smile, nice-guy vibe.

"When Stephanie told me about your walk, I was hoping we'd be able to meet up. I'd like to walk with you, too, if it works out. We can talk over dinner," he says opening the car door.

When we've settled in the car, I lean forward from the back seat. "What, exactly, constitutes 'Wisconsin food' around here?"

Dave looks at me in the rearview mirror. "There's a place over nearby to get walleye and potato pancakes with applesauce. That's good Wisconsin food."

Remington's River Inn sits with its back up against the Milwaukee River, and looks like it's been there for a century or so, a living piece of history. We walk through the heavy, wooden door and then through a long, arched hallway studded from floor to ceiling with rounded river rocks. The hostess seats us at a thick, wooden table.

Dave and Stew – I keep reminding myself to say "Stephanie" around Dave – catch up on family news for a bit, then the talk turns to the lake.

"So, how has this adventure changed you?" Dave asks.

"I'm certainly in better shape," I laugh. "It's been a luxury to have unbroken time to contemplate things: the lake, the environment, my life, even. This adventure has reshaped me inside, too. I feel like I'm recording the lake in my body. Like it's becoming part of me."

The fish is excellent, like they were wriggling earlier this day. It begins to rain and we listen to the drops hitting the deck outside. "Have you hiked in the rain a lot?"

"Only a few days, and only an hour or so each time. Out of 52 days total now."

"That's incredible," he says.

Dave is the President of the Board of Directors at the Schlitz-Audubon Nature Center that is located on the lakeshore. We coordinate to meet him there for the last day's hike into Milwaukee, then Dave drops us back at the hotel.

Falling in

The next day proved to be the most challenging of this segment. We continued the trek by walking through Harrington Beach State Park. The brick kiln where they fired the limestone still stands on the property along with the foundations of workers' houses. The quarry is now a 60-foot deep, crystal clear, circular lake.

From the park, we headed south along the rocky beach, often with a limestone shelf extending into the lake under the waves.

At Port Washington, we take a jog inland to get around the harbor. Then we continued south past another power plant to the Lion's Den Nature Preserve where we once again accessed the lake. We had to descend to the lake down a bluff, on stairs maintained by the preserve.

As we continued south, following the bluff, I noticed that it was mostly red-brown clay that had eroded to a sheer wall in many places. It was certainly not something we would be able to climb, but I wasn't worried because our ending point this day was at a university that had developed a stretch of their shoreline; I knew they had installed a steep, paved path with many switchbacks down to the lake.

The beach was rocky and the going slow for the first few miles, then we found ourselves scrambling over felled trees and darting between waves to get around obstructions. At one point, I skirted a cluster of tall trees with grip-sized trunks leaning out into the lake. Stew was behind me, and she must have used one of the branches for support because I heard a big *crrrraaack!*

I turned and saw her falling backwards into the water, the treacherous branch still clutched in her hands. As she splashed backwards under a wave, I stepped into the water, grabbed her hand, and hauled her out.

"Are you hurt?" I asked as I dropped my pack and pulled out a chamois towel.

"Just wet," she said.

I held the towel out flat and said, "Electronics!"

She looked at me a moment, then handed me her wet camera.

"Phone, too."

I popped them open, pulled out the wet batteries, and wedged the chamois into the battery space. Then, I wrapped it all up in the towel. I pulled out a dry shirt and gave it to Stew.

On my trek, I had had a lot of time to contemplate what I would do if I fell into the water. Saving my GPS, camera and phone seemed like a smart thing to do. All of her electronics survived the plunge. The day was warm enough that getting doused wasn't a problem, and I was just glad she wasn't hurt.

The beach expanded and contracted for a bit, then slowly shrunk down to a sliver filled with downed trees and brush. We took a break on the top of a pile of logs we had to climb, and I pulled out some chocolate-covered espresso beans. By this time in the trek, this was my go-to snack when the going got rough. We chatted for a bit and caught our breath before pressing on.

A short walk from our break, we came across a dead and munched-upon eight-point buck, its ribs stripped of most of the meat while the head and neck were still intact. This was a big buck to take down. And once again, I wondered what was out here that could do such a thing.

Along this stretch there were places where the breeze coming off the land brought the overwhelming smell of cow manure. Wisconsin's license plate declares it is "America's Dairyland," so it is only logical that there would be quite a few bovine hanging around. It was a little mind-boggling, though, to contemplate how many thousands of cows had to be in close proximity to the lake in order for the smell to be that strong on the shore.

Milwaukee holds the unique distinction of being the site of the nation's largest documented waterborne disease outbreak in history. In 1993, *Cryptosporidium* from cattle waste passed through the filtration system of the city's water-treatment plant, and over 400,000 people were infected. Judging from the strength of that smell along the shoreline north of Milwaukee, I wouldn't be surprised if waste was still entering the lake, especially after heavy rainfalls.

Before walking each segment, I would study maps, then satellite images from Google Earth. From the images, I could see where there was beach and if there was exposed rock along my route. What these photos couldn't tell me is how high the rock was stacked, or if the lake was higher or lower than the level it was when the photo was taken.

This day, that information mattered. We hit a place a few miles away from our exit path with huge, intentionally placed chunks of rock. I had seen this on the photos and had noted it on my map with the comment "placed rock – walk around? Wade around?" When we got there, it was clear that the rock was placed in very deep water in order to keep the steep hillside from sliding into the lake.

We scrambled up and above the rock and around the bend. We could see the hillside with the switchback path off in the distance, but in between was an area where the hillside had sloughed off into the lake, leaving a nearly sheer face of clay dropping off into deep water. In addition, the water was filled with algae and fallen trees. We had no way forward.

Luckily, the hillside right above us stabilized by the rock was covered with vegetation. Even though it was quite steep and high, we were able to scale it without it falling away beneath our boots. We trudged our way up and out and back to the roads and made it to the north side of Concordia University's campus.

It began to mist on us as we waited for Phil to pick us up, but only began to rain once I had stowed my walking stick in the trunk. It had been a 21-mile day, and one of the most challenging I had encountered on the Lake Trek with all of the climbing up and over and through obstructions, and with Stew's lake baptism.

Schlitz-Audubon Nature Center

The final day began at the Schlitz-Audubon Nature Center where we met up again with Dave. Bob Bailie, the marketing coordinator, gave us a tour of the modern center. The Dorothy K. Vallier Environmental Learning Center opened in 2003, and boasts the use of natural ventilation, passive solar heating and cooling, and was built with a good deal of recycled materials. It is heated with a geothermal system, using 90 groundwater wells and the warmth of the earth, instead of fossil fuels.

The center also houses one of the few "nature preschools" in the nation. The school welcomes nature into the classroom and curriculum. A fort inside was constructed with tree branches, and an old, bent tree with many looping branches served as a play structure outside. It looked like a great place for kids to get their knees dirty, to catch a grasshopper to study the surprised look in its eyes.

The center owned a stretch of shoreline, so after the tour the three of us hiked down to the lake and headed south to Milwaukee. The lake was riled up, mud-colored from stirred-up sediment, and waves crashed up high on the beach. Dave lived between the center and Milwaukee, so he served as our guide.

The lake, however, did not cooperate and much of the way where Dave said there was usually beach, there was none. We found ourselves climbing up on rocks for much of the morning, crouching under branches, and getting our boots doused by errant, massive waves. I mistimed the waves once and found myself standing in water up to my knees. When that happens, there is no longer any pressure to keep your boots dry, so I slogged on regardless of the rhythm of the waves. We took to streets for impassible parts, but mostly stayed on the rocks until we reached the city of Whitefish Bay.

Dave found the path that led up to his house, and he brought out refreshments while we caught our breath on the deck and twisted water from our socks.

By this point, we were teasing there's-beach-just-around-this-point Dave about how well he knew his stretch of the lake. It goes to show how changeable the lake is, from year-to-year and even day-to-day.

Stew was back in her boots this day, but they were not holding up to the rugged hike. She thought back over the times and places she had worn them and had determined they were over 20 years old. When we emerged from the wilderness and into the parks along Milwaukee's north side, Stew switched into her hiking sandals and was seriously considering tossing the boots.

When we saw a garbage can, she untied them from her pack, extracted the still-usable insoles and laces, posed for a photo, and let the boots go. It was difficult for her.

We passed the Milwaukee Art Museum with its winged Calatrava-designed addition. Then, we walked past Discovery World on the waterfront, a museum dedicated to educating people about the Great Lakes and the oceans. The facility also boasts the mobile classroom tied to the pier alongside the building: a 137-foot, three-masted Great Lakes schooner, the *Denis Sullivan*. A skilled crew built the boat with the help of over 1,000 volunteers. The boat is docked in Milwaukee during the mild months, and is sailed through the Great Lakes, then south along the east coast to spend the winter months in Florida.

Dave got us down to the river in Milwaukee, then to a restaurant with outdoor seating where our rugged appearance didn't offend other patrons. I was able to pull off most of the clinging seeds from my pants before our food came. After lunch, Dave had his son, Charlie, pick us up, and they drove Stew and me back to cover the remaining 7 miles between the nature center and Concordia University where we had finished the day before.

The sun was setting by the time we got to the entrance of the university. We had, again, hiked 21 tough miles.

The next day Phil and I would board the lake ferry to cross the waters again and head home. That day happened to be my birthday. Stew remembered and had her sister – who was picking her up at the hotel – bring baked goods and a candle, and they sang to me. I was touched, and thankful to have had her always cheerful and chatty presence at my side for this rugged stretch of the lake.

I arrived back home in time to continue my birthday celebration with Jim, Ben, and Lucas. That night, I heard Jim talking to his cousin on the phone.

"No, all the way around. It's about a thousand miles. She's already done over 900."

A pause, then he chuckled. "I know! I have a hard time getting to the gym twice a week! It's amazing."

I caught his eye and he smiled at me.

Mackinac Bridge Walk

September 7
St. Ignace to Mackinaw City
6 miles

Total Trek Mileage: 917 miles

Spanning the Straits

Labor Day is the only time foot traffic is allowed on the Mackinac Bridge. So, I backtracked to connect this missing piece of the trek, the span across the Straits of Mackinac on the Mighty Mac.

With only the final segment of the Lake Trek remaining, it felt strange to go back Up North to territory that I had covered over a month ago. Jim and Lucas joined me on this quick excursion. We packed up the car on Sunday afternoon and strapped on Ben's bike and a few things that didn't fit into his car when he'd returned to college. After dropping Ben's things off in Grand Rapids and taking him out to lunch, we continued north and drove over the bridge to the city of St. Ignace where we stayed the night.

The bridge was completed in 1957. At that time, it was the longest suspension bridge in the world. The feat of building a bridge across the Straits of Mackinac was, for a long time, considered to be impossible. The structure would have to withstand the strong currents in the deep water (over 300 feet deep in one glacial groove), not buckle under the pressure of the winter ice that can be up to four feet thick, and also resist the winds that can scream through the straits at over 100 mph. The fact that the bridge was built at all is an engineering marvel; that it was done in a time before the tools of modern engineering – like computers and GPS – almost qualifies as miraculous.

I'd driven across the bridge many times and was always struck by its beauty. Where the Brooklyn Bridge is all broad shoulders and brawn, the Mighty Mac is grace and sweeping lines. Its two simple towers rise over 500 feet above the water and lift up the middle section of the bridge like a woman hiking up her long skirt so as not to get it wet. The creamy white towers have a simple pattern cut in them that gives the bridge an elegant Art Deco feel. These holes serve more than a decorative purpose, though, since they give the winds a portal through the towers. The bridge is five miles long, contains a half million cubic yards of concrete, more than a million steel bolts, and around five million steel rivets. The cables holding up the roadway are comprised of over 42,000 miles of skinny wire, all bound together into cables six feet in circumference.

I was looking forward to placing my boots on the bridge, to enjoying the view, and even to walking on the open grating of the road surface where a piece of perforated metal would be the only thing between me and the water far below.

We stayed in a hotel a mile from the bridge, and began walking to the starting point after breakfast. The morning was foggy and warm, and once we were on the bridge we could see only 100 yards in front of us. The first tower was shrouded behind the thick fog. We joined the stream of happy walkers and moved at the pace of the crowd up the incline toward the first tower. The fog slowly swallowed the bridge behind us, so we were soon moving on a section of the bridge surrounded by fog. We couldn't see the water for the first part of the walk, and it was an ultra-calm day so there were no sounds of water moving against the bridge supports that plunge up to a hundred feet into the lake bedrock.

National Guardsmen directed traffic and walkers, and every school bus in the area is used to shuttle people back and forth. Many walkers were pushing people in wheelchairs. For some, the bridge walk was a tradition they had done their entire lives, so they continued even past the point of being able to walk it. Since it is only five miles, it doesn't require walkers to be in amazing condition, so there were people of all shapes, sizes, and fitness levels. There were a surprising number of people smoking while they walked. Many wore flip-flops. One guy was barefoot.

We saw the cables begin to rise in the fog on either side of us well before we saw the first tower. It was surreal to walk the bridge essentially in a cloud. After we passed the first tower, the fog seemed to descend.

Or, maybe it was the additional rise of the road between the towers that elevated us above the fog. We could finally see land on the other side, and the fog hovered on the surface of the calm water below.

While walking, there was time to study bolts and rivets, to get a sense of the girth of the cables swooping to the top of the towers, to look down through the metal grating to the water far below. The straits were virtually glassy; I had never seen them so placid. When I'd taken the ferry to Mackinac Island with Phil and my boys just two months earlier, the captain of the boat said we could sit on the open, upper deck of the boat, but we would get "bathtub wet." Not sure exactly what this meant, we started the ride up there. Then, as the boat plunged into the troughs between waves slapping giant walls of water onto us, we got his meaning and scurried down the stairs into the protected deck of the boat.

The fog began to burn off as Jim, Lucas, and I made our descent past the second tower. It was windless, though, and muggy, and I was glad we had brought water along with us. A Coast Guard boat patrolled the waters parallel to the bridge, and the waves it made were the only disturbance on the water.

When we crossed the finish line in Mackinaw City, we were each handed a certificate saying we had walked "The World's Greatest Bridge."

You should be in the hospital

Ten days before the beginning of the last segment of the trek, I had a horrible backache that tossed me out of bed in the middle of the night. That was followed by what I thought was the worst case of stomach flu *ever*. In between bouts of hurling, I kept counting the days until the next segment. As the horribleness kept going – the fever, the hurling, the stomach and back pain unlike anything I had experienced – I was reduced to counting the days on my fingers. *Ten days, I could recover from this in ten days, no problem.* Two days later, I was still fighting my way back to health and planning for the final 100 miles and celebration in Chicago when I noticed that the whites of my eyes had yellowed.

I hated to go to the doctor, but having yellow eyeballs wasn't something I could will myself to get over. Jim drove me to urgent care, and then over the next few days I saw an internist, had an ultrasound, and saw a surgeon. They pulled many tubes of blood and prodded and poked me.

Turns out my gall bladder attacked me. Well, they call it a gall bladder attack, and that's what it felt like. A gallstone was making its way down the bile duct and got stuck. In the process, it riled up my pancreas. Trust me, you don't want to rile up your pancreas. If you fear getting attacked by your gall bladder, be even more afraid of an angry pancreas.

"I'd like to admit you," my surgeon said.

"She's not sick enough to be in the hospital," Jim said unhelpfully.

My surgeon looked at my lab results. "Yes, she is. I'm surprised she's functioning at all with these labs," she said to him, then looked at me.

"You must have an extremely high pain tolerance."

I explained to her that I was going to finish the Lake Trek in a few days, so whatever had to be done, they'd better do it quickly. They scheduled a procedure to "retrieve the gall stone endoscopically." That sounds elegant, but it means that they put you out and put a tube down your throat, through the stomach, into the small intestine, then go up the common bile duct and pluck out the offending stone.

The procedure went smoothly, and the stone was one of the biggest the doctor had ever removed. I felt pretty good even before they pulled it out, and felt even better once it was gone. They used the "Michael Jackson drug," Propofol, to put me out.

I expected to get woozy, to drift away, but it was more like *WHAM!* Lights out. One minute I was on the table, looking at the doctor holding the lighted scope, the next I was being wheeled down the hallway to the recovery room.

Segment 10

September 21-26
Milwaukee to Chicago
102 miles in 6 days

Total Trek Mileage: 1019 miles

Walk it off

Four days after having my gallstone removed, I drove myself 2 1/2 hours north and caught the lake ferry one last time to Milwaukee to begin the final segment. I had forced myself to rest in preparation for the final 100 miles, and now just reclined my seat during the crossing and closed my eyes for a bit.

It was difficult. I was excited and worried about holding up on this final stretch. It seemed rather cruel to have gotten into such good shape – I'd dropped over 20 pounds and put on a lot of muscle – only have my gall bladder and pancreas double-team me at such a crucial time.

When I got off the ferry, I decided that it was time to walk it off, to stretch my legs, get moving toward Chicago. The ferry docked south of downtown Milwaukee, and I began walking through a series of parks.

This first day of Segment 10, the lake was placid, calm and quiet. The ferry crossing had been smooth and fast. When the wind blows, the lake finds its voice. Its waters murmur or speak up or shout or scream depending on the power of the waves. I've walked the shoreline when the enormous waves made a crashing, crushing sound as they hit the beach. It was deafening.

This day was the antithesis of that one. Rarely is the lake without some sort of wave action, if only a gentle lapping on the rocks, but this day it was silent, a flat mirror to the softly smudged, gentle sky.

I walked the first few hundred yards just feeling how my legs were moving, trying to regain the rhythm of the trek. I felt a light sweat forming on my back where my pack rested against my body. The day was mild and a little muggy, but the warmth felt good. Not far from the ferry dock, I met up with a friend of mine, Philip, who lives in Milwaukee.

Walking with a person who loves the lake had become one of the joys of the trek for me by this point. Philip and his wife live in an old working-class neighborhood, Bay View, on the south side of Milwaukee.

As I walk past the south marina, I see Philip sitting on a bench. I lift my walking stick in greeting, and he rises.

"I'm so glad you had time to walk with me today," I say.

"Me, too," he says. "It's too nice to be inside all day."

Instead of staying on the shore, he leads me up a slope to a massive beech tree. The tree is in a lakeside park, and even though there are many mature trees everywhere we look, this beech stands apart. This giant specimen has been rooted here for over 150 years. A plaque near its base labels it "Wisconsin's Largest European Copper Beech Tree" and puts its height at over 60 feet.

Beeches have skin-like bark, smooth to the touch. This massive specimen's bark stretched over its muscular torso. The tops of this ancient tree's roots have erupted from the soil like it's sprouting feet. The gray bark is wrinkled in places, and every split or name carved into it becomes a prominent tattoo. It looks like an elephant took root and grew leaves. The shadiest side of the trunk is covered with a scrim of moss. At its base, I'd estimate it would take at least four people – maybe five – holding hands to encircle its trunk.

I look up to its crown of green leaves.

"Thanks for showing this to me," I say as I rub my hand along a smooth part of its trunk. Since I always try to stay as close to the water as possible, I would have missed this magnificent tree.

"We only have a few beech trees in Wisconsin, just along the edge of Lake Michigan where the winters are milder."

He leads us off to the south, but soon after the park, as the shoreline turns into a high bluff, he's ready to take another little detour, through a seminary named for St. Francis.

"Behind the seminary is a bit of old-growth forest."

The Catholic institution has been there since the mid-1800s. Mature maple trees line the paved road to the black-domed building, with a statue of St. Francis in front, looking out at the lake. We wander behind and through an old cemetery filled with rows of humble, low tombstones for all the nuns who have died there.

"My wife's great-aunt lives in the Sisters' House here," Philip says. "It's like a retirement home for old nuns."

"I had a great aunt who was a nun," I remember. "Sister Assumpta. Very 'old school' with the habit and black dress. She used to scare the hell out of me and my siblings when we were little."

We walk the loamy path through the old woods. An enormous hollow tree had recently fallen. "There was an owl who nested there last year," Philip says, looking at the shattered trunk on the ground. A few paces further, we see a fawn, still young enough to wear its spots, then see its mother. The doe allows us to pass her within arm's length.

It's a remarkably quite, peaceful place.

He leads me back out to the path along the lake bluff. "Tell me something interesting about your stretch of the lake," I say.

"Well, I can tell you an important piece of Labor Union history that happened here in the Bay View neighborhood in the late 1800s. There was a city-wide workers' strike demonstrating for the 8-hour workday, instead of the common ten to twelve hours. The workers organized a march to close down the last factory open in the city, the Bay View Rolling Mills, and the militia opened fire on them.

"I think around ten workers were killed, mostly Polish. It was called the Bay View Massacre. Same issue as the Haymarket Massacre in Chicago, and it occurred at exactly the same time. These lakefront factory towns were full of immigrant workers, and they were just starting to organize for better conditions."

"Wow," I tease, "no happy stories?"

I mull over this bloody piece of history on the lake as we walk the pathway south. We climb as the bluffs get even higher, with wonderful views far out onto the lake and back to the Milwaukee downtown skyline, silhouetted across the bay. We pass by clusters of wildflowers in bright colors along the trail, a bike path that hugs the lake.

"Well, I need to leave you here," Philip says. "Those condos up ahead are part of a lakefront redevelopment. There used to be an old power plant here, I think. They built a new one down near Oak Creek and tore this one down."

"Thanks for the grand tour," I say.

We hug and part.

Jenny Appleseed

I pressed on alone. I hadn't told him about my medical saga, wanting instead to focus on the lake. The first miles had gone smoothly; I had found my rhythm. The wildflowers were in riotous blooms on the bluff falling off into the lake. Thistle and goldenrod, asters and chicory all showed their festive colors. The leaves on the trees were beginning to change and even to fall on this last full day of summer.

I began my trek in March during the last days of winter, had hiked through the spring and summer and would end it in the fall having walked in all four seasons. I had seen the lake with ice along its eastern shore, had waded it during the chilly spring, then cooled off in its waters during the summer, and would now watch the leaves falling onto its glassy surface.

I continued hiking south on the paved path and diverted off onto dirt trails when they ventured closer to the water. A fat toad was hopping alongside one of these paths, and I gently caught him up just to look into his black eyes lined in copper.

I crossed Oak Creek on a stone bridge. On a sidewalk further on, an elderly man passed me on one of those scooter things. As he zipped by he called out, "Where are your apples? You look like Jenny Appleseed with that big walking stick!"

DAVE GIVES OUT THE ROOMS!

I finish the day's hike at a small motel. I had called to make a reservation, but the man who answered always shouted "DAVE GIVES OUT THE ROOMS!" So, I show up, hoping Dave will be there.

After ringing the doorbell, then knocking on the office door for several minutes, a tiny, ancient, hunched man wearing a white shirt and dark pants held up high by burgundy suspenders tentatively opens the door.

"I'd like a room. For one night, please."

"WHAT?"

Realizing he is almost deaf, I raise my voice. "I'D LIKE A ROOM FOR ONE NIGHT, PLEASE."

"DAVE GIVES OUT THE ROOMS!"

"OKAY. CAN I GET A ROOM FROM DAVE?"

"DAVE'S NOT HERE!"

"WHERE IS HE?"

"TRY HIS HOUSE!"

"I DON'T HAVE A CAR. DOES HE LIVE CLOSE BY?"

The gnome-like man points vaguely through the motel. "DAVE LIVES OVER THERE."

"DO YOU HAVE HIS ADDRESS?"

He waves me in to the office and says, "I'LL SHOW YOU. WATCH YOUR STEP!"

Amazed that the gnome man could still climb stairs, I follow him down to the cluttered, musty basement. He unlocks the four locks on the basement door and opens it. Just across the back parking lot is a tiny white house.

"GO TO THE SIDE DOOR. SEE IF DAVE'S THERE."

I walk the fifty feet to Dave's house and knock and ring the doorbell. I wait and repeat. Dave isn't there, so I walk around the front of the motel to find a place to sit. When I get to the front, there's Dave, scurrying around to get a room for "me and my husband," a guy who arrived in a big, red pickup.

I explain to Dave that we aren't together, and the pickup guy, a young man wearing jeans, a T-shirt and baseball cap, explains that he needs a room for three weeks because he is working at the new power plant. The pickup guy has the disturbing habit of clicking his teeth together after every sentence, like he can't help it. Or like he had just come off an ecstasy high. He returns to his truck, and Dave lets me in the office.

The gnome man is back inside the little apartment beyond the office. He sits with his knees almost touching the screen of his gigantic console television. His chair is so overstuffed that it looks like it is in the process of swallowing him.

"Only one night?" Dave seems puzzled.

"Yep. Do you have a non-smoking room?"

Dave stops his scurrying. It's obviously a new question. "No. No." His eyes light up. "But I have my emergency room! It hasn't been used in a long time!"

This sounds a little scary. Exactly what emergency had taken place there?

I follow Dave into the little hallway to the very first room. He opens it up, hustles inside and flips on the window AC unit. "How's this? This'll do?"

"Sure." I'm too exhausted to walk much further anyway. Dave hands me the key and heads back to the office. I close the door behind him and slip the chain into the slider. Then, I turn to look at the room again.

I've stepped back into the '60s. Ashtrays as big as my head take up every horizontal surface. The lamps and furniture look like props from an Austin Powers movie, the bedspread is a mod pattern in bright orange, and the paneling is dark fake wood. The thing that really pulls this horror together is the artwork: a large, semi-impressionistic oil painting of a matador and bull.

I am, after all, in small-town Wisconsin – but through what time machine did I travel to this place?

Exhausted, I drop my pack on the second bed, then unlace my boots and extract my tired feet. After scooping all the pillows onto one bed, I recline on them and turn on the TV. I relax while watching the national news before braving whatever moldy horrors might be revealed in the bathroom of this "emergency room."

The bathroom is surprisingly decent, tiled floor to ceiling (including the ceiling) in little multi-colored square and rectangle tiles. I take a long, hot shower. The increased humidity revives two obese flies who attempt to fly up to the light. I kill one with a snap of a towel, but the other one escapes into the room, buzzing like a saw chewing through a chunk of oak. It lumbers for the old light fixture between the beds and I pursue, snapping the towel.

The brittle light-shade fractures, and the fly buzzes inside. A few more whacks finally fell the behemoth.

I turn the cracked part of the shade to the wall, slide the chair up under the doorknob to the outside, turn off the light and tumble into a deep sleep.

Electricity comes from the lake

The first thing I passed the next day was the new Oak Creek power plant where the young guy at the hotel was now employed. It was a hazy morning, so its structure was shrouded in mist. I had passed many power plants along the lake by this point in the trek. I hadn't given electricity much thought in the past, but now I was seeing up close where it was produced.

I walked by long strings of coal cars brimming with black chunks extracted from the mountains of Wyoming. I saw the mini-mountains of coal nestled near each plant, and skirted the coal ash retaining ponds from which the Creature of the Black Lagoon would likely emerge.

I had read about the recent Kingston, Tennessee, coal-ash spill. When the wall of a retaining pond burst one billion gallons of black muck were discharged into the Emory River and the valley below. The images from helicopters over the scene were horrific: houses enveloped in muck – some swept off their foundations by the force of the flow – a clear river turned black and chunky.

It wasn't too far south of the plant that I was able to descend a small hill to the shore. This was where I always felt the happiest, that place where the water lapped at my boots, where I could have a conversation with the lake. The beach along this stretch, a few miles north of Wind Point, was narrow. Mature willows dotted the shoreline, their tendrils rustling in the mild lake breeze.

Wisconsin law allows people to own the land right to the water's edge, so I walked in that band of land that the waves were keeping wet. This zone – and the lake – is still considered public.

Rock walls and houses of light

Soon, I came across a series of rock jetties placed along the property lines so that each house had their own walled beach. On satellite images, these jetties were visible. What I couldn't see from space, though, was that many of these walls were taller than me, some of the individual boulders larger than refrigerators.

Strolling on the beach – even a rocky one – isn't very tough, but having to scale a series of moist, rock walls is quite a workout. Some of the jetties were wide, too, so I had to balance and hop my way across gaps on the top of them.

I took many breaks along this stretch. Avoiding fatigue meant avoiding mistakes or missteps that could mean an injury, I thought, just as my boot slipped off, then down between two boulders. My calf banged along the sharp edges before my boot wedged in the gap. After extracting my leg, I lifted my pant leg and saw only a light scrape on my calf.

Toward the end of the series of fifteen jetties, I saw a man standing on one of the rock walls. I waved to him, then eventually climbed up to stand next to him.

"Do you live on the lake?" he asked.

"No, I'm walking all the way around it. Is this your house?"

"No. I'm the engineer who placed these rocks. I'm inspecting them."

"Well, they're holding up fine," I smiled. "I've been over them thoroughly. Now I know who to curse when I have to climb over the rest of these," I laughed, gesturing to the walls farther down the beach.

We discussed the shoreline beyond Wind Point, and he told me about areas I would not be able to walk. South of the lighthouse, he told me, I'd have to take to the roads again since there was no beach and, often, just long, steep stretches of jumbled retaining rock trying to secure the steep shoreline.

This man had placed a lot of rock to stabilize the Wisconsin lakefront.

It's always exciting to find a lighthouse along the beach. They seem like old friends as they emerge from behind the trees or out of the mist. I'm sure that sailors felt – and still feel – that same connection to these beacons, even today when most of the lights are no longer lit. After walking over 900 miles of shoreline, I had developed affection for these reassuring sentinels, too.

The Wind Point Lighthouse is one of the tallest on the lake at just over 100 feet, and is one of the few the Coast Guard still lights to guide ships in the night. The grounds were groomed and flowering. I took a break on a bench near an iron capstan once used to manually raise and lower a ship's anchor. Dark clouds were conspiring, so I slipped on my rain gear.

By the time I left the lighthouse, it was pouring. Up to this point in the trek, I had, amazingly, been rained on for probably 5 hours total, spread out over several days. I certainly could not complain, and this rain didn't last more than an hour.

The road hugged the lake in places, and at one public access I watched a man hoist a white kayak onto his shoulder and walk down a path to a launch site between two piers. His racing kayak was extremely skinny and tapered to a long, narrow point in the back and with a hooked, fin-like rudder near the tip. It had a well in the middle that he straddled in the shallows before jumping in. Stroking the boat swiftly through the breaking waves, he passed the piers and proceeded out into the vast lake beyond. Soon, I could barely make him out between the rolling, mounded waves.

It wasn't too much farther that I entered the city of Racine, with its zoo right along the lakeshore. I stopped in to visit the animals and had the place pretty much to myself.

It was strange to hear the sounds of the lake mix with the roar of a lion.

Leaving the zoo behind, I walked the wide, public beach, then scooted past the wastewater treatment plant and the marina. Crossing over the Root River, I entered the quaint and quirky downtown. When I got to the inn where I would stay the night, my scraped-up calf was throbbing. When I lifted my pant leg a massive black-and-green bruise was revealing itself.

The next day I walked through the city's Southside Historic District. Houses were built here between the mid-1800s to the 1920s. The large area, 42 blocks in all, displayed "a variety of Greek Revival, Victorian period, and Prairie School architectural styles," according to the official marker. Notable architects such as Racine's own Lucas Bradley and the more famous and mercurial Frank Lloyd Wright, also a Wisconsin native son, had designed some of these lovely homes.

The path most often taken in Kenosha

A few miles farther, approaching the north side of Kenosha, I found the Pike Bike Path that runs for several miles through parks along the lake. A woman who had been following my adventure online, Susan, had emailed me, offering to walk her hometown of Kenosha with me. I called her when I found the path, and she confirmed she'd meet me in a few minutes.

Up ahead is a skinny woman with salt-and-pepper hair and a small pug dog on a leash. She's letting him drink from the faucet on the bottom of a drinking fountain. When she looks my way, I lift my walking stick in greeting.

"You must be Susan," I say as we shake hands. "And this must be Burlee."

I kneel down and pet his square little head. He looks at me with his bug eyes and smushed-up face.

We walk toward downtown. "Kenosha has a lovely lakeshore," I say.

"The city finally realized what an asset the lake was in the last decade. Before that, it really hadn't developed the shoreline," Susan says.

"Why not?"

"Kenosha had been a strong manufacturing city, but those jobs were mostly exported in the 1990s, leaving the city with abandoned – and sometimes toxic – stretches of land and fewer jobs. The city has cleaned up many sites, including where the American Motors factory stood on the south side of the river. They cleaned that site up and built condos. That's where my husband and I live."

"Right on the river?"

"Yes, we're nearly there," she says as we walk the bridge that bisects the marina. "The city figured that they could attract tourists from Chicago if they put parks along the lake and a marina for sailboats." The Harbor Park area is indeed attractive, with public meeting spaces, parkland, a museum, and slips for motorboats and sailboats alike. Once again, it seemed that cities on the lake were rediscovering what an incredible asset they had . . . if the lakefront was kept clean and welcoming to locals and visitors alike.

The park even has an electric streetcar line, a 2-mile loop linking the harbor with downtown and the Metra station, where commuters can catch rapid transit to Chicago.

This day is the longest of this segment, so I am delighted that Susan has time to chat over snacks at her condo.

"How about crackers and cheese? I'm sure I have some Wisconsin cheddar," she asks as she heads toward the kitchen.

"Perfect!" I take off my pack and settle in a chair. Burlee comes over and I scratch his funny square head again and find that special place behind his ear. His eyes roll back.

"It's probably a law in Wisconsin that you have to have cheese in the fridge at all times," I joke.

She brings out a platter and gives me a serious look. "How did you know that?"

We laugh. We both have backgrounds in medical research, and Susan is also a writer, so we have many common interests to explore while Burlee waits for a piece of cracker to find its way to him.

Susan walks with me a bit after our snack. She gives me a tour of the small museum row along the river – the natural history museum and a Civil War museum.

"Reclaim and Revitalize" should be the city's motto. I was happy to see a city making such good use of its waterfront.

Susan waved goodbye and I began walking again, through the huge homes holding their ground on the hill overlooking the lake on the south side of Kenosha. Soon, I'm entering the Chiwaukee Prairie area. The Chiwaukee is a preserve of over 500 acres of wet-mesic prairie. There are over 400 species of native plants due to the diverse habitats within the tract of land. It is a haven for all kinds of wildlife, too. There were several vacant lots on the lakeside of the prairie that were maintained for public access, and I took a break at one of them. The day was warm, so it felt good to extract my feet from my boots and cool them in the clear, lake water.

It wasn't too far after leaving the Chiwaukee that I crossed the state line between Wisconsin and Illinois. I felt like I was truly in the home stretch of the Lake Trek. I finished almost 24 miles this day. The hotel had rooms with Jacuzzi tubs, much my delight. After working the kinks out of my body in the deep tub, I tossed in my sweaty clothes and used my walking stick to stir them around until they were clean.

Nature preserve, or toxic Superfund site?

The next day I hiked out to the Illinois Beach State Park. The wet prairie habitat continued here, and over the tall grasses I could see the top of the Zion Nuclear Power Station. This plant was taken offline in 1998.

This park is unique in several ways (besides having a nuclear power plant nearby), including being credited as "the first formally dedicated nature preserve in the world," according to signs in the park. The habitat is diverse, ranging from dune and swale to marsh, sedge meadow and *panne*. Panne – which I had not noticed previously – is a rare wetland near the lakeshore dominated by twig rush and blue-joint grass.

When I studied the maps of this area, I had decided to hike the shore-line of the park down to a coal power plant where I'd return to the roads. There were signs in the park, though, warning that the area south of Dead River was a nature preserve accessible by permit only.

I follow the signs to the ranger station. The glass door is plastered with signs warning people that *Proper Attire Is Needed To Enter The Ranger Station* and *Do Not Track Sand Into The Ranger Station* and other warnings that pretty much obscure the view into the small building.

I enter, expecting to find at least three rangers there in pressed uniforms, taking their duties ever-so-seriously, but find the reception area staffed by one woman, and she is on the phone.

"Do you know what they named her? Amadora Maria!" she exclaims. "No, he's not Italian, they just liked the name. It means 'the gift of love.'"

I politely thumb through the pamphlets, moving around enough so I am sure she has seen me. She continues to chat for the next twenty minutes. I explore every pamphlet and map in the place, then stand and gaze out the wall of windows onto the lake, hoping she'll finally run out of the minutia in her life to discuss.

I'm about to leave when she finally hangs up. I stroll over to the desk and stand there for another minute while she studies her nails. The world turns a little bit more. She finally comes over to the counter where I'm waiting.

"May I help you?" she asks.

"I like to get a permit to hike past Dead Creek."

She roots around under the desk and pulls out an application. "Fill this out and mail it to Springfield," she says, and I remember that Springfield is the capital of Illinois.

"I'd like to hike it today," I say. "I've hiked over 970 miles so far, almost around the whole lake. I'm on my way to Chicago now, where I started."

She looks less impressed with this than if I had told her I had named my kids Dimitri and Sven even though I'm neither Greek nor Swedish.

"You'd have to talk to the ranger, then."

"Sure," I say, expecting her to call them from the back office.

"He's at a meeting but will be back soon."

Exasperated, I give her my cell number and tell her I'll hike down to Dead River and wait for his call. On the way out, I am pleased to note that even though I had stomped and wiped my boots, I have still managed to track a little sand onto the tile floor.

The wide beach was deserted except for a gathering of gulls. It was an easy hike down to Dead River where I sat on the sandy bank to wait for the ranger's call. The Dead River is more like a pond snaking its way through the prairie. A wide sandbar blocked the connection to the lake.

Illustrated signs warned that while the river flowed very slowly, it could build up pressure and could explode through the sandbar, rushing out into the lake.

That sounded exciting, but I was pretty sure I was in no danger from Dead River on this warm, fall day, since the area had been in a drought most of the summer.

While waiting, I studied my maps and questioned if I'd be able to make it to the road near the power plant, or if wetlands would block me once I had walked the miles through the nature preserve. That would mean I'd have to backtrack, something I hated to do. I had also noticed from satellite images that there was an old industrial site between Dead River and the power plant, situated up against the nature preserve.

After almost an hour, I decided to hike back out of the park instead of waiting any longer for permission.

Later, I found out that the old industrial area was where a Johns-Manville plant once stood, a designated Superfund site. It was heavily contaminated with asbestos before the location was cleaned up, then sealed over with dirt. By this point on my trek, I was no longer surprised by these stories, but I always felt a deep sadness that the lakefront had been so abused and still held such lasting wounds.

There is something lonely about prairies and wetlands. Maybe it's the expanse that your eye can look across at the level of the tall grasses. The land seems remote since it is shrouded in rustling, swaying plants. I'd walked through areas like this and it was difficult to know when the land would give way and envelope your boot – or entire leg – in muck. I'd seen places where deer had bedded down for the night, circles of tall grass pressed down under their resting, warm bodies.

The trail took me back out to the park's main road, but I veered off of this onto a dirt track. It ended at a tall chain-link fence. As I was taking off my pack to toss it over, I noticed that the fence to my left had been cut and pulled open in a perfect little doorway. Thankful that I didn't have to climb, I slipped through the exit, walked past an abandoned, trash-strewn camp for the homeless, then through the nearby trailer park, and out onto a main road heading south to Waukegan.

A toxic legacy

While Kenosha had a small clean-up to do along the mouth of its river, Waukegan had a massive one. Nancy A. Nichols' book *Lake Effect: Two Sisters and a Town's Toxic Legacy* chronicles her family's very personal experience with Waukegan's toxic history. I had read this book prior to walking this stretch and had sworn to myself that I wouldn't be drinking the lake water in Waukegan!

The water never really was the problem here, though. PCBs were the problem. Several industries – especially the Outboard Marine Corporation – dumped these into the river, contaminating the sediment. PCBs are not water soluble, but they will accumulate in fish and animals. The fatty coho salmon is the perfect, top-of-the-food chain repository for these fat-soluble chemicals. So perfect that in 1969 the FDA had to seize and destroy tens of thousands of pounds of coho from the lake because they were too toxic to eat.

Three separate Superfund sites were designated in Waukegan in the 1980s. Two are along the lake, and one is a nearby landfill. One of the lakeshore sites was the Johns-Manville factory that was located next to the power plant. The restricted "nature preserve" was surely a buffer to keep people away from it.

I walked south toward the power plant that I had seen in the distance from Dead River. I turned onto a rough and little-used road lined with coal cars and power lines. Power plants are zoned to have a large buffer of undeveloped land around it. It's not uncommon that such plants erect fancy signs designating the surrounding area as "nature preserve."

In my pre-trek research, I had come across an Environmental Release Profile Report for coal-fired plants in Michigan. In it is a table with columns of numbers expressing how many pounds or tons of things like sulfur dioxide, carbon dioxide, acid gases, mercury, arsenic, chromium, and nickel are released from each plant annually.

For instance, the lowest annual emission of sulfur dioxide is "only" 355 tons by the plant in Marquette County. The plant in Monroe, Michigan, has the highest at over 100,000 tons. Annually. That plant also expels 651 pounds of mercury. Annually.

The report also estimated that there are almost 2 million children living in the thirty-mile zones around these plants.

As I walked the road near Waukegan's plant, I thought about electricity. How vital it is, but also how high an environmental price we are paying with these coal-fired plants. Why can't we – as a society – see the long-term value in paying more for developing green energy in the short term?

Since industry uses around 80% of the energy produced in Michigan, why can't the state give tax credits to industries that become more efficient in their usage, like the government gives to home owners who insulate their houses?

Why not encourage green buildings for industry and homes, give tax incentives to use alternative energy sources, and fund research into improving the harnessing of winds, waves, and sun and making nuclear power safer?

I encourage anyone who thinks that coal is the way to go for the future to walk by the plant nearest you. You won't be able to get that close due to the buffer zone/nature preserve, but you'll get close enough to realize that maybe tearing up the land for coal, transporting it over 1,000 miles using diesel trains, then burning it up for energy – with all the toxic by-products that creates – may not be the most intelligent, sustainable way for us to get power.

The buffer zone near Waukegan's plant had grown into a wild mass of plants and trees and vines. It amazes me that nature will persist in the most inhospitable areas. Along this rotting road near a belching power plant and industrial areas with toxic legacies, I saw many kinds of birds flitting about, two garter snakes, monarch butterflies, and a riot of wild flowers in bloom.

Walking south to the harbor, I passed through active industry to the marina where I took a break to look out at the lake.

I had walked through so many areas that had a toxic relationship with the lake. I had left boot prints along the shoreline in Montague, past Green Bay's Fox River, and now along Kenosha's and Waukegan's harbors.

It amazed me what harm humans can do to such a vital and immense body of water, how little foresight was involved in the actions taken over decades, over generations, to virtually destroy an ecosystem that is so large it would take over 64 days to walk around. To pollute one of the world's largest sources of clean water. To negate the benefits of living close to the lake for ordinary people, instead to offer industries a place to dump waste.

And how, with the stroke of a pen – as with the Clean Water Act – much of the malevolence could be brought to a screeching halt.

I had heard the *we didn't know it was harmful* defense given by many of the executives responsible for allowing industrial waste to be dumped into open fields or rivers or the lake.

Well, they didn't take even the most basic measures to determine if it was harmful, did they? How many of those executives allowed their own children to play in the dumping fields or swim in the river where they dumped PCBs, benzene, asbestos, and the other soupy mix of toxic chemicals their plants produced?

South of Waukegan, I passed through the city of North Chicago. I wove my way through neighborhood streets to get off the busy main road, but I noticed many people sitting in their cars with the engines running along these side streets. It was a mild day, and I wasn't sure what to make of this. It started to feel unsafe, so I returned to the main road.

There I saw a new public-service campaign poster on the side of a building. It had a photo of a forlorn little boy. The slogan, presumably something the little boy was thinking, was "Don't shoot me, I want to grow up!"

It was part of something titled a new "Ceasefire Campaign."

I kept walking.

The Navy on the lake

There is a naval academy located on Lake Michigan. "Naval Station Great Lakes, Quarterdeck of the Navy" was emblazoned on each gated and guarded entryway. This 1,600-acre facility has been on the lake for almost 100 years. President Teddy Roosevelt signed the order for its construction. As I walked the bike path along the black, metal fence, I could hear the recruits singing in cadence as they jogged on training runs.

A bike trail, the Robert McClory Path, would take me all the way to

Lake Forest where I would stay the night. It passed through some lovely rural stretches and some small towns, like Lake Bluff and Libertyville.

Since the lakeshore was not accessible, I started on the bike path on the second-to-last day of this segment. The path was an easy place to walk, but I soon felt isolated from both the lake and the communities, so I veered onto a road closer to the lake where I hoped to at least catch glimpses of blue water.

I turned toward the lake into the historic town of Fort Sheridan. This town was a military base, from the late 1800s when it supplied troops for the Spanish-American War all the way through Desert Storm in the early 1990s. Now there are plans to put a golf course on the parade grounds. There are interpretive signs throughout the nature preserve and the city proper, giving its history. There were photographs of the troops riding horses and marching in formation on the grounds.

In one photo, a young soldier stands on his head, his legs out to the side at right angles to his body, while another soldier jumps a horse over him.

I caught glimpses of blue water through the trees and turned south again on roads as close as possible to the bluff overlooking the lake.

I walked roads through Highland Park, then found the path again and walked it all the way to Winnetka. Sheridan Road south of Winnetka stayed close enough to the shoreline that I could smell the water at times. There was also an occasional park where I could descend to the lake.

It was along this stretch on Day Five of this segment (Day 63 overall) that I reached the 1,000-mile mark.

I walked down to Elder Lane Beach and then out onto a pier. The waves were curling, splashing water several feet into the air when they struck the pier. I stood on the very end, watching the waves rush by on either side, enjoying the feel of the droplets hitting my face and bare arms.

I thought about how far I had come.

The day was hazy. Chicago's skyline – though less than 20 miles away – was hidden. I thought back to the beginning of the trek, in March. How Chicago's skyline recede behind me as I made my way south along the bottom of the lake. Now, it would emerge from the haze to greet my return from the north.

I finished the few miles to my hotel in Evanston, took a long shower, and waited for my sister Leslie and cousin Milene to arrive. They were going to stay the night with me and then walk the final day of the Lake Trek. Since Les and Milene were ten-mile people, I had planned this last day to be within their comfort zone.

Besides, I wanted to end the last day with a smile on my face.

My phone rings about 6:30 p.m. Les says that they will arrive soon. I hang up and organize my things. I'd been throwing out my most worn clothing along this last part of the trek, and now I am reduced to the clothes on my back. This has allowed me to travel light for this last segment.

I am exhausted and sore. The gallstone saga has taken far more out of me than I care to admit, and these last three days were all walks of around 20 miles each. As I limp down the stairs to wait for their arrival, I am indeed glad that the final day will only be ten miles. I'm sure I'll have energy for the celebration we've planned to follow my arrival on Navy Pier.

It begins to rain as I wait. I retreat inside and take a seat on some white marble stairs and look out on the street. There will be around 40 people who will gather at the end of the Lake Trek. I think about friends and family making their way to Chicago, about new friends I've made on this adventure who will be there, and others who just love Lake Michigan like I do and want to greet me and celebrate the completion of this journey.

When Les and Milene arrive, I use the handrail to stand, then hobble outside to greet them in the rain.

"This is going to be so great! Where are we going to dinner? This rain better stop! I'm so excited! Carry this! Are you excited? " They chatter over each other, as usual, and I smile, grab some of their stuff, and guide them inside.

"Oh, this is nice! How long have you been here? I'm so excited!"

"Let me show you our room," I offer as I guide them to the elevator. We settle in and I change into some fresh clothes that Les brought with her, then we go to the hotel's restaurant for dinner. It is an elegant, old-world Italian place, and I plan to carb load for the final day.

"Are you excited?" Milene asks.

"Yes. But it's kind of hard to believe it will be finished tomorrow."

"And Ben's walking with us?" Les asks.

"And some of his friends. Jim and Lucas hope to arrive, too, in time to walk the final couple miles." I pull out a birthday card and slide it across the table to Milene. "Happy birthday."

"That took some planning to hike for days with a card," she says.

"Sorry it's a little smushed," I laugh.

After a fantastic dinner, we settle into our room. I take the pull-out couch since Milene suffered sleeping on one the last time they hiked with me, and Les and Milene share the massive king-sized bed. When we wake in the morning, both of them confess to not sleeping very well since they slept on the opposite side they were used to.

Realizing that they could have swapped sides and slept well, they crack up laughing.

Keep the lake on your left

That final morning, we wait at a park. A taxi pulls up and Ben, his room-mate (also Ben), his girlfriend Mary, and two other friends, Christie, and Becca, spill out. It's like a clown taxi for college kids.

As we begin walking south to Chicago, I turn to the kids and in my most serious voice say, "Keep the lake on your left." They just stare at me.

"Really. If it's on your right, you're going the wrong way."

When Ben smiles, I crack up, and they all laugh.

The morning is still a bit hazy, so the skyline reveals itself in increments as we cover the final ten miles to Navy Pier. We walk wide beaches for much of the way, and terraced concrete blocks along the curve of the lake, and paved pathways around marinas.

Our group stretches out along the shore and I find myself having time to visit with individuals as they appear at my side and match my stride. They all get around to asking me how it feels to be so close to the finish. Finally, walking within this group, I allow myself to fully consider the completion of my adventure. I've been so focused on getting through the five days leading up to this point, concentrating on building my stamina again, falling exhausted into bed each night, that I haven't taken much time to consider fully that my trek is coming full circle.

"Great," I find myself answering.

Then, "Fantastic. It feels fantastic."

As the skyscrapers emerge from the haze, I find myself grinning, knowing that the end is near, that more friends and family and people who love the lake are that moment gathering to celebrate. People were coming from Georgia, North Carolina, Indiana, Illinois, Kentucky and Michigan for the Lake Trek Celebration.

Chicago is one of my favorite cities in the world, and I get a little choked up when the John Hancock Building finally shakes the fog from its big shoulders. Sandburg's poem rings again in my ears, *Chicaaaoooogoooo*. Stretching out into the lake I can see Navy Pier, the beginning point of my adventure which will soon serve as its ending.

Jim and Lucas join up with us about a mile from the end. I hug Lucas, then turn to Jim. He takes me in his arms, and I hug him back.

"Thanks for coming," I say.

"Wouldn't miss it," he replies and squeezes me tighter. "Feeling okay?"

"Yep."

I get giddy with anticipation as we begin walking the length of the pier. This is the very place where I took the first steps of the Lake Trek over seven months ago. It was deserted then, early in the March morning. Now there are crowds of people wearing shorts and T-shirts, music streams from the speakers, the kiosks are staffed, the restaurants crowded. It smells like fried food and fun.

We make our way past the Ferris wheel, then out toward the far end. There, a group forms a large semi-circle. When I see them, I lift my arms over my head, lofting my walking stick. I wave and a cheer rises, and they break into applause.

Many hugs and tears follow.

There is a moment during the celebration when I slip away from the crowd and walk to the very edge of the pier. The music and noise falls away as I concentrate on the movement of wind on the surface of the lake, the gentle noise of the water swirling through the pilings of the pier.

On that edge, I look to the south and see again the tendrils of smoke now swept back over land. I look east and retrace that sandy shoreline in my memory. I look north to the limestone shelf wilds of the Upper Peninsula, and then west to the clay cliffs and tangled deer paths I have walked.

1,019 miles after the beginning, I have arrived at the end, having come full circle.

I realize that the long list of reasons for taking this journey was obscuring the underlying motivation for my quest: to be alone for a time. It was a test to see if I could move through the world on my own, to see if I still liked who I am at my core. While I treasure the time on the lake with family and friends, the majority of it was solitary, navigating my way, looking always forward, moving toward that singular goal of encircling the lake with my footsteps. I had time to see what stores of resolve and strength and courage resided within me. Time to be fully alive, solitary, and completely present in the moment.

And, at the end, I found I was content and confident within myself.

I rejoined the celebration, renewed.

Epilogue

I had walked over 1,000 miles. I felt younger, stronger, more sure of my step and stride. It was a gift to myself, this adventure. Time to get to know "my lake" and to get reacquainted with my true self.

And now, with this book, this trek is my gift to you. What challenge will you take on in your own life? What are you passionate about? Who are you at your core? Are you too busy looking into the past or future to be alive in the moment?

I encourage you to find those things and take them on, to launch out on an adventure to find yourself, be it on a weekend or weeks, be it a few miles or a thousand.

Live your life as an adventure.

Acknowledgements

An adventure of 1,000 miles is not accomplished without assistance. I am in debt to many people who allowed me to ask questions, cheered me on, transported me to the lake, walked by my side, housed me along the way, or gathered to greet me at the end.

Thank you to the experts who took the time to enlighten me about the lake: Joel Brammier, President of the Alliance for the Great Lakes, Tom Kelly, Executive Director and Captain of the Inland Seas Education Center, and Dr. Deanna Van Dijk, Aoelian Geomorphologist and Professor at Calvin College. I was inspired and informed by Jerry Dennis and his books and essays about the Great Lakes.

My brother, Phil, was the primary Lake Trek Transporter who shuttled me to and from the lakeshore. My friend and fellow writer, Vickie Weaver, met up with me around the city of Green Bay and shuttled me to and from the bayshore for several days. There were several times on the trek where I needed a lift and relied on the kindness of strangers. Thanks to the steelworker who gave me a ride to the hotel that I could see, but not walk to, to the sympathetic kayaker who gave me a lift into Glenn Arbor, and to the father and son on their way to a baseball tournament in Battle Creek who gave me a ride home from the ferry in Ludington.

Though I walked alone for eighty percent of the Lake Trek, there were a handful of enthusiastic people who met up with me and walked a few hours or days at my side. I am thankful for their energy and for the conversations about the lake that we shared. In order of their appearance on the shoreline, they are: Ben and Lucas (my sons), Mary Vermeulen, Leslie Shipley, Milene Plisko, Theresa Rugel, Rick Land, Gerry Sell (along with her dogs Miss Sadie and the Cowboy), Susan Remson (and her dog Burlee), Stephanie Lyon, Lois Otten, David Hoover, and Philip Martin. For the last ten miles into Chicago I was joined by my son Ben and his friends: Mary Healy, Cristine Hromada, Ben Verhulst and Becca Farnum. Leslie and Milene also walked the final ten miles because they are "Ten-Mile People." My husband, Jim, and son Lucas joined us for the very last mile.

A special thanks to my husband, Jim. Though he was dubious in the beginning, he was with me at the end.

I am constantly thankful for Spalding University's MFA program and all the wonderful people associated with it. A special thanks to my mentors, Robin Lippincott, Phil Deaver, Mary Yukari Waters, and Rachel Harper. Sena Jeter Naslund, founder and director of the program, is a goddess. The program's staff, Karen Mann, Kathleen Driskell, Katy Yocom, and Gayle Hanratty, are the heart of the program.

In addition, I am thankful to those who took the time to read early versions of this manuscript and to give thoughtful comments. Much gratitude to Vickie, Juyanne, Maija, Theresa, Phil, Les and Milene. And to Robbie for helping me with the PR during the trek.

A big thanks to all the kind people I met along the lakeshore that share my love of Lake Michigan. A special joy was visiting many of the independent bookstores along the lakeshore.

A list of these stores follows, and I encourage readers to support their local independent bookstores.

A huge thanks to everyone who gathered at the end of Navy Pier on September 26, 2009, to greet me at the last of my 1,000-Mile Walk on the Beach. I will forever remember that moment and your smiling faces.

Bookstores Visited

Of all the kind people I met along the lakeshore that share my love of Lake Michigan, I especially enjoyed visiting many of the independent bookstores along the lakeshore.

I encourage readers to support their local independent bookstores, as special places where literature, regionalism, and community come together to celebrate where we live and what we care about.

Unabridged Bookstore, Chicago IL
Women & Children First, Chicago IL
The Bookworks, Chicago IL
Sandmeyer's Bookstore, Chicago IL
57th Street Books, Hyde Park IL
Powells, Hyde Park IL
Quimby's, Chicago IL
Barbara's Bookstore, Chicago IL

Forever Books, St. Joseph MI

Black River Books, South Haven MI
Singapore Bank Bookstore, Saugatuck MI
Readers World, Holland MI
Treehouse Books, Holland MI
The Bookman, Grand Haven MI

Book Nook & Java Shop, Montague MI

The Bookstore, Frankfort MI
Dog Ears Books, Northport MI
Brilliant Books, Suttons Bay MI

Horizon Books, Traverse City MI
McLean & Eakin Booksellers, Petoskey MI
The Island Bookstore, Mackinaw City & MackIsland MI
True North Books, Mackinaw City MI

Book World, St Ignace MI

Frigate Books, Gladstone MI

Bayshore Books, Oconto WI
LaDeDa Books & Beans, Manitowoc WI
Next Chapter Bookstore, Mequon WI

Book Stall at Chestnut Court, Winnetka IL
Lake Forest Bookstore, Lake Forest IL

Organizations
Working to Protect the Great Lakes

These are some of the leading organizations working to protect the Great Lakes. They are worthy of your support and of your active efforts to understand their work, to gain some understanding of the crucial issues that they are tackling, and to pass the word on to others.

Individually, we can do only a little; together, we can make a real difference in the quality of life for us, our children, and future generations.

Alliance For the Great Lakes
   http://greatlakes.org/

Great Lakes Echo
   http://greatlakesecho.org/

Great Lakes United
   http://www.glu.org/

Healthy Lakes.org
   http://www.healthylakes.org/

Sierra Club
   http://www.sierraclub.org/

Related Reading

Annin, Peter. *The Great Lakes Water Wars*. Washington: Island Press, 2006.

Ashworth, William. *Great Lakes Journey: A New Look at America's Freshwater Coast*. Detroit: Wayne State University, 2000.

Brown, Grant. *Ninety Years Crossing Lake Michigan: The History of the Ann Arbor Car Ferries*. Ann Arbor: University of Michigan Press, 2008.

Dennis, Jerry. *The Living Great Lakes: Searching for the Heart of the Inland Seas*. New York: Thomas Dunne, 2003.

Grady, Wayne. *The Great Lakes: The Natural History of a Changing Region*. Vancouver: Greystone Books, 2007.

Nichols, Nancy A. *Lake Effect: Two Sisters and a Town's Toxic Legacy*. Washington: Island Press, 2008.

Smith, Carl. *The Plan of Chicago: Daniel Burnham and the Remaking of the American City*. Chicago: University of Chicago Press, 2006.

Steinman, David & John Nevill. *Miracle Bridge at Mackinac*. Grand Rapids: Eerdmans, 1957.

Wille, Lois. *Forever Open, Clear, and Free: The Struggle for Chicago's Lakefront*. Chicago: University of Chicago Press, 1991.

Additional Links

Videos of my Lake Trek adventure

Videos of each segment of my adventure are live on YouTube.
http://YouTube.com/LNiewenhuis

Blog of the Lake Trek and current news, book events, etc.

The blog of my adventure with many photos is at:
http://LakeTrek.Blogspot.com

Statistics from the Lake Trek

Number of miles total:	1,019 miles
Days on Trek:	64 days
Average miles/day:	16 miles
Longest day:	25 miles
Shortest day:	5 miles
Percent of trek walked alone:	80%
Longest Segment, #7:	10 days to hike 161 miles
Shortest Segment, #4:	50 miles
Number of pairs of boots worn:	3 pair